GREATER YELLOWSTONE

Fly Fisher's stream guide

Ken Retallic

Ken Retallic (signature)

GBH *ink*

Idaho Falls, Idaho

Traveler's Companion Book

Published by
GBH *ink*
190 S. Corner
Idaho Falls, ID 83402

ISBN 0-9652775-0-X

Printed in USA

Cover photo: Sunset on Henry's Fork by Ken Retallic
Jacket design: Ken Retallic and Jerry Painter
Inside photo, maps: Ken Retallic

Portions of this book previously appeared in different form in "Fly Fisher's Guide to Idaho," The Post Register, Intermountain Hunting & Fishing, and Streamlines.

Also available from GBH *ink*:
"Fly Fisher's Guide to Idaho," Ken Retallic and Rocky Barker, 1996, Wilderness Adventures Press, Bozeman, MT.

To Eugene K. Retallic Sr.

Thanks Dad for that long ago canoe trip down the Allegheny River when we were in the Boy Scouts together. Little did we know it would evolve into a life-long fascination with sparkling clear waters.

■

"In the whole region (the West), mere land is of no value. What is really valuable is the water privilege."

John Wesley Powell,
Green River, Colorado, April 1877

■

A book like this is not possible without the generosity of friends and experts who share a similar love for sparking clear waters and their inhabitants. At the risk of forgetting to name a few, I thank Bruce Staples, Jimmy Gabettas Sr., Jimmy Gabettas Jr., Mike Lawson, Bob Jacklin, Richard Parks, Bill Schiess, Rob Thornberry, Rocky Barker, Jerry Painter, Herb Pollard, Mark Gamblin, Steve Elle, Bill Schroeder, Lynn Kaeding, Bob Meseroll, Dale Withington, Jack Parker, Michael Vadnie, Chuck Haga, Bernie Kuntz, and Michael Graham, who built my first fly rod.

Charles E. Brooks and his seminal books, "The Living River" and "Nymph Fishing for Larger Trout," brought me to the Intermountain West to stay. I salute him and hope he continues to watch over us from his camp fire in the Milky Way.

I also thank retired Post Register publisher Rob Brady, who made it possible for me to come to Idaho. His friendship, kindness and generosity are incomparable. He embodies the true pioneering spirit of the West and its residents who love all our wild creatures, great and small.

Table of Contents

Larry Schoenborn, left, host of the television program "Fly Fishing the West," plays a cutthroat on the South Fork of the Snake in eastern Idaho. South Fork Lodge outfitter Spence Warner rows and Curt Gowdy, well-known outdoorsman and broadcaster, continues to cast during a filming episode in 1991. (Photo by Ken Retallic)

Introduction

Welcome to the Golden Circle of Trout

Preserved in 1872 "For the benefit and enjoyment of the people," the world's first national park is today the heart of the largest intact north temperate ecosystem on Earth. Pilgrims flocking to Yellowstone number in the millions. Its geothermal wonders are second only to its teeming herds of wildlife, flights of birds and schools of fish. For fly fishers it's nirvana. Stretch the boundaries of Yellowstone almost 100 miles in all four directions and you find an opulence of exemplary cold water fishing unmatched outside of Alaska. I call it the Golden Circle of Trout.

Actually elliptical in shape, the Greater Yellowstone Ecosystem extends from Bozeman on the north to St. Anthony on the west to Cody on the east to Afton on the south. Seven national forests encircle Yellowstone and Grand Teton national parks — the Gallatin, Beaverhead and Custer in Montana; Shoshone and Bridger-Teton in Wyoming; Targhee and Caribou in Idaho. Combined, the parks and forests provide a concentration of public lands access unique in the Lower 48. Greater Yellowstone harbors almost 2,000 miles of trout streams. About 1,000 miles follow serpentine courses through the parks. The other half meander through the people's forests.

Arterial flows from the headwaters of the Yellowstone Plateau and contiguous snow-capped mountains straddling the Continental Divide drain north and southeast to the Atlantic, south and northwest to the Pacific. Among these legendary rivers of the Intermountain West are the Yellowstone, Snake, Henry's Fork and South Fork of the Snake, Madison and Firehole. Less renowned but noble equivalents are the Fall, Teton, Boulder, Gallatin, Lamar, Gibbon, Bechler, Salt, Grey's, Hoback, Gros Ventre, Clark's Fork of the Yellowstone and North Fork of the Shoshone. Stillwater treasures hallowed in fly fishing annals are Yellowstone Lake, Henry's Lake, Shoshone Lake, Heart Lake and the alpine gems of the Beartooths.

First dips into this cornucopia of blue-ribbon trout waters are best made with specific destinations in mind. Always budget extra time to explore. Be prepared for provocative challenges from the rivers' finned beauties. The trout are wild and wary, but often remarkably accommodating. This guide and its maps direct you to key starting points to the fly fishing adventures of your dreams. To help them come true, the data on each stream include principal aquatic insect hatches, effective fly patterns, river characteristics and flows, boat ramps, public access sites, seasons and special regulations. Other tips suggest worthy side trips or points of interest. For additional help getting started, all the major rivers and lakes are serviced by expert outfitters, guides and well-stocked fly tackle shops. A directory of phone numbers and addresses is provided at the back of this guide.

How to use maps

The Greater Yellowstone Ecosystem, known to fly fishers as the Golden Circle of Trout, is big. Covering 18 million acres, it is larger than West Virginia.

Many first-time visitors to the West are not prepared for the scale of its geography. All western states are considerably larger than states east of the Mississippi. The Intermountain West's terrain further contributes to longer travel times between destinations than first anticipated. Its lush river valleys dissect spectacular mountain ranges and dramatic canyons.

Schedule ample road time whether you plan a weekend trip or an extended vacation. Like its meandering rivers, there are no straight roads in Greater Yellowstone — although, seemingly for the fly fishers' convenience, the majority of the region's roads follow long stretches of its rivers. This is good or bad, depending on your viewpoint. But the trout are just as wild at roadside as they are in the region's backcountry retreats. Separate road maps for each state are recommended.

Maps accompanying the stream data are not drawn to scale, but river mileage references are included to permit realistic planning of float trips or wading explorations. In essence, they are highlighted enlargements of professional maps available from the U.S. Forest Service, the National Park Service and commercial sources. Landmarks recorded on the enclosed maps stress the better locations to fish and public access sites like boat launch pads, maintained side roads and public campgrounds.

Foot trails have not been recorded for two reasons. The lower reaches of most of the region's rivers are paralleled by public highways, county roads or forest roads. Public access sites outside the parks or forests are marked by highway signs by each state's fish and game department. Trailheads within the parks and forests are well marked, and on short hikes you can confidently follow the directional signs along the trails. For ventures into wilderness areas, it would be prudent to consult regional hiking guides and topographical maps, or hire a guide.

In Greater Yellowstone, it is possible to fish more than one river in a day. However, it is more productive to stick with a river for two or three days and explore more than one stretch. A rule of thumb to follow on all Western rivers is that if there's no action in an hour or two, move on to another place. Some streams fish better in mid-morning or early evening. This usually depends on seasonal hatches as well as current weather conditions.

Mountain weather patterns often change quickly and dramatically. Pack for early spring or fall-like conditions even in mid-summer. Include rain gear or a windbreaker, a sweater, extra wool socks and waterproof matches or a lighter in your day pack. Always carry a water bottle or canteen. Don't forget insect repellent, sun screen lotion, polarized sunglasses and a hat.

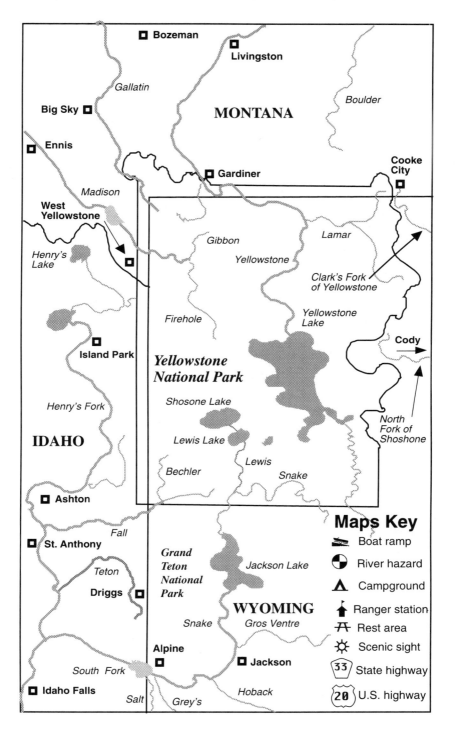

Bozeman

Livingston

Gallatin

MONTANA

Boulder

Big Sky

Ennis

Cooke City

Madison

Gardiner

West Yellowstone

Gibbon

Lamar

Yellowstone

Clark's Fork of Yellowstone

Henry's Lake

Firehole

Yellowstone Lake

Cody

Island Park

Yellowstone National Park

Henry's Fork

Shosone Lake

North Fork of Shoshone

IDAHO

Lewis Lake

Bechler

Lewis

Snake

Ashton

Fall

St. Anthony

Grand Teton National Park

Jackson Lake

Teton

Driggs

WYOMING

Snake

Gros Ventre

Alpine

Jackson

South Fork

Idaho Falls

Hoback

Salt

Grey's

Maps Key

🛥 Boat ramp

◑ River hazard

▲ Campground

⬧ Ranger station

🛧 Rest area

☼ Scenic sight

(33) State highway

(20) U.S. highway

Yellowstone National Park

Fountainhead of West's best wild trout streams

As an environmental barometer gauging the aquatic health and stability of the Northern Rocky Mountains, the cutthroat trout is like the canary in a mine.

Only remnant populations of this vulnerable, colorful native trout survive in the Intermountain interior, restricted to the headwaters of some of the West's greatest rivers. Its largest stronghold is Yellowstone National Park, where the Yellowstone cutthroat reigns supreme. But even here, where pristine waters still run cold and clear, the threat of environmental disturbances from outside the park remain a clear and present danger.

A potentially disastrous threat to the park's cutthroat was discovered in 1994 when lake trout were found in Yellowstone Lake. This illegal transplant of a predatory non-native species could eventually destroy the cutthroat fisheries in the lake and upper Yellowstone River. Yellowstone's guardians are trying to find solutions to this peril. Anglers are required to help by killing all lake trout caught in Yellowstone Lake and Heart Lake.

Without the stricter fishing regulations imposed in 1973 on Yellowstone Lake and Yellowstone River, the park's preeminent cutthroat citadels would have been hard pressed to survive the continually increasing hordes of anglers plying their waters. In 1987, officials extended the catch-and-release restriction to cutthroat and rainbow trout in all but a few of the park's streams. A two-cutthroat-under-13 inches bag limit was continued on Yellowstone Lake and its tributaries. Grayling were given catch-and-release status years ago. In 1996, the rules were changed again to further protect native cutthroat and permit a limited take of non-native species in most of the park's waters.

Under current regulations, cutthroat are catch and release on all park waters, except Yellowstone Lake and its headwaters drainage. Daily creel limit on rainbow trout is two fish any size park-wide, except for four key rivers. Rainbows are catch and release on the Madison, Firehole and its tributaries, the Gibbon below Gibbon Falls, and the Bechler River. Creel limit for brook trout is five fish any size, except in Richard's Pond, Fawn Lake and Blacktail Ponds, where it is five brookies under 13 inches. Brown trout creel limit is two fish under 13 inches on the Madison, Firehole and Gibbon, below its falls. Elsewhere in the park, the brown limit is two fish any size. Lake trout limit is two fish any size in Lewis and Shoshone lakes.

Yellowstone became a lead-free fishery in 1994. The ban against using lead sinkers, split-shot, or lead-weighted flies and jigs was imposed to protect trumpeter swans and other waterfowl from lead poisoning.

Cutthroat provide up to two-thirds of the angling pleasures in the park, primarily on Yellowstone Lake and Yellowstone River. The most crowded water in the park is the Yellowstone River; 80 percent of its more than 22,000 annual anglers flock to the nine-mile stretch below the lake. Still, U.S. Fish and Wildlife estimates that more than 70 percent of the Yellowstone's one-day anglers land one or more cutthroat. The catch rate is one fish per hour; average size is 15 inches, and 24-inchers lurk here.

Due to its gullibility, many anglers may catch the same cutthroat. An Idaho State University study found that each cutthroat tagged was caught an average of 9.7 times per season in the upper Yellowstone River. Catch-and-release mortality rate was estimated at 3 percent. The upper Yellowstone supports more than 7,500 fish per kilometer (.6 mile). Fish and Wildlife notes that because of biomass restrictions, the increasing number of larger fish may decrease the population and eventually the catch rate. But it says anglers will still be able to rely on the "recatchability" of cutthroat.

This is not a guaranteed phenomenon. Larger cutthroat are not nearly as gullible as their younger brethren. All sizes exhibit degrees of selectivity when they single-mindedly key on only one insect species or stage of a hatch. Late-summer and autumn anglers will find plenty of challenges to match-the-hatch.

If crowds are not your game, dip into the Yellowstone's canyon stretches; rainbows are found below Lamar River, browns below Knowles Falls in Black Canyon. To get far off the beaten track explore its headwaters.

A gargantuan, percolating geologic sponge, Yellowstone Park gives birth to a host of venerable wild trout rivers. The Madison and Gallatin are two of three tributaries that form the Missouri River. They join the Jefferson at Three Forks in Montana. The Snake River, largest tributary of the Columbia, flows through western Wyoming and into Idaho. Its flows are augmented by the Lewis River. The Madison is formed by the merger of the Firehole and Gibbon rivers. Bechler River merges with the Fall River, which flows into the Henry's Fork in eastern Idaho. Flowing into Montana to join the Missouri, the Yellowstone's major tributaries in the park are the Lamar and Gardner rivers. Clark's Fork of the Yellowstone and North Fork of the Shoshone rise just outside the park's eastern border.

Slough Creek, a tributary of the Lamar, is the best of the bewitching mountain meadow streams in the park. Two tributaries of the Lamar, Soda Butte and Pebble creeks, are very popular with families who want to practice their fly casting skills on small rainbows and cutthroat. They have the highest catch rates in the park. Other small fish havens include Fan and Specimen creeks in the Gallatin drainage.

Held in reserve strictly for children are the brook trout of Panther, Obsidian and Indian creeks. The Gardner River and these three tributaries are the only park waters open to bait fishing by children. Reserved for fly fishing only are the Madison, Firehole and Gibbon, below its waterfall.

Madison River

BEST FEATURES: Large multi-faceted river that bestows a variety opportunities and challenges to fly fishers. Second in renown only to the Yellowstone, it flows through a picturesque valley teeming with wildlife.

SEASON: Saturday, Memorial Day weekend until Loop Road closed.

REGULATIONS: Fly fishing only; rainbow, catch and release; brown trout, 2 under 13 inches.

TROUT: Resident rainbows and browns in upper river mostly in 10- to 15-inch range, some up to 24 inches; stronger populations and larger fish in lower stretches. Big rainbows move up from Hebgen Lake to spawn in spring and follow browns on fall spawning run, which extends up to waterfalls on Gibbon and Firehole. Some browns weigh in at 5 to 10 pounds.

MILES: 150 from Madison Junction to confluence with Missouri River, including 23 miles in park. Mile 0: Madison Junction. Mile 5: Nine Mile Hole. Mile 7: Seven Mile Bridge. Mile 8: Grasshopper Bank (Long Riffle). Mile 14: The Barns (Riverside). Mile 18: Beaver Meadows. Mile 23: Baker's Hole.

CHARACTER: Madison manifests as a quintessential trout stream with merger of Firehole and Gibbon rivers in National Park Meadow. From flats below Madison Campground down through Nine Mile Hole, the river twists and turns in long sweeping curves, undercut banks, channelized pools and intermittent riffles and runs. Avoid the marshy area extending about a mile above Seven Mile Bridge; thick layers of silt in river make wading hazardous. Flow quickens below bridge, where weedy channel above Grasshopper Bank turns into long rumpled riffle as river veers away from loop road. Famous holes and runs of The Barns are below Cable Car Run near Riverside Road parking lot. Downstream, river flattens and meanders through marshy Beaver Meadows in long pool-like glides divided by side channels, broad riffles and narrow runs. Baker's Hole is just across park's boundary.

FLOWS: Spring runoff usually peaks by June; relatively moderate most years, but it can run over banks in wet years. Muddy runoff of Gibbon sometimes turns river off-color into July. Firehole's flows warm upper Madison.

ACCESS: Loop road follows top half of river for about 10 miles. Turn off to lower river is 1 mile east of West Entrance. Beaver Meadows also can be reached by faint trails north of West Yellowstone from Baker's Hole Campground or from U.S. Highway 191 pullout across from Airport Road.

HATCHES: Stone fly, golden stones, late-June, July in fast waters; green drake, June, early July, and Trichos, August, in slow waters and Beaver Meadows. Basic mayflies, caddis through season; terrestrials after mid-July.

FLIES: Stoneflies, 4-8; green drake,10-12; BWO, PMD, Adams,14-18; Tricho,18-22; elk hair caddis, humpies, stimulators, Wulffs,12-16; ants,14-18; beetles, 10-14; hoppers, 8-12. Hare's ear, prince, pheasant tail, soft-hackle nymphs, Zug bug,12-18; dark stone, woolly bugger, streamers, 2-8.

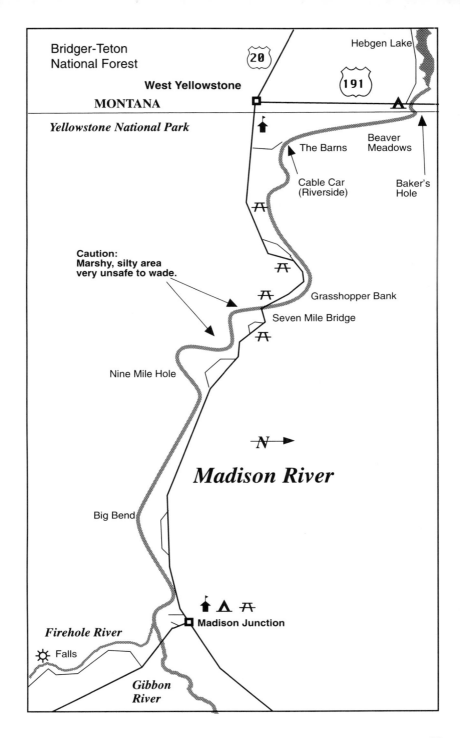

Bridger-Teton
National Forest

Hebgen Lake

20

West Yellowstone

191

MONTANA

Yellowstone National Park

The Barns

Beaver
Meadows

Cable Car
(Riverside)

Baker's
Hole

**Caution:
Marshy, silty area
very unsafe to wade.**

Grasshopper Bank

Seven Mile Bridge

Nine Mile Hole

N

Madison River

Big Bend

Madison Junction

Firehole River

Falls

*Gibbon
River*

Gibbon River / Grebe Lake

BEST FEATURES: Classic mountain meadow dry fly stream above tumbling pocket waters stretch that plunges over scenic 84-foot Gibbon Falls. Its source, Grebe Lake, harbors grayling; most popular small lake in park.

SEASON: Saturday, Memorial Day weekend through October 31.

REGULATIONS: Fly fishing only below Gibbon Falls; 2 rainbows above falls, catch and release below falls; 2 browns under 13 inches below falls; 5 brook trout. Grayling catch and release in Grebe Lake; 2 rainbow limit.

TROUT: Rainbows up to 17 inches and grayling in Grebe Lake. Pan-size brook trout, a few small rainbows in outlet and meadows above and below Virginia Cascade; fair-sized rainbows, some lunkers, and brook trout in Elk Park and Gibbon Meadows; larger rainbows and browns below waterfall. Madison River's brown spawning run extends up to Gibbon Falls in late-fall.

MILES: 38 miles; Grebe Lake to Virginia Cascade, about 10 miles; cascade to Norris Junction, about 5 miles; junction to Elk Park, about 3 miles; Elk Park to end of Gibbon Meadow, about 5 miles; meadow to waterfall, about 10 miles; falls to Madison, about 5 miles.

CHARACTER: Lake outlet a small mountain stream that spills off Mirror Plateau to short meadow before dive down Virginia Cascade, and then meanders through Norris Geyser Basin. Solfatara Creek and geyser outflows double river's volume through Elk Park and Gibbon Meadows, where it cuts across a broad flat in a serpentine course marked by deceptively deep pools and heavily undercut banks. River then gallops down a narrow canyon filled with pocket waters and churning runs to Gibbon Falls, where a plunge hole often holds large trout. String of rocky riffles and swift runs continues to short meadow stretch about a mile above Madison Junction.

FLOWS: Easy to wade in moderate, stable flows after spring runoff ends, usually by July. Runoff peaks earlier and flows can get very low by autumn in drought years. Some meadow channels very deep; fish from bank.

ACCESS: Madison-Norris road parallels much of river through canyon and parts of the flats. Better fishing in upper and lower meadows is to hike in away from road. Hike to Grebe Lake, from Norris-Canyon road, is 3.5 miles.

HATCHES: Good dry fly stream even though mayfly hatches relatively minor. Watch for brown drakes in upper meadow in June, early July. Full length of river look for Baetis in early spring and late-fall; PMD and caddis, starting in June; ants, beetles and hoppers, mid-July through September.

FLIES: Brown drake, 8-10; BWO, blue dun,PMD, Adams, 14-18; elk hair caddis, humpies, stimulators, renegades,Wulffs, 12-16; ants, 14-18; beetles, 10-12; hoppers, 8-12. Hare's ear, prince, pheasant tail nymphs (including beadheads), 10-14; large nymphs, woolly buggers in fall for browns below waterfall. Grebe Lake: small nymphs, mayflies for grayling; Adams, caddis, Wulffs, black or purple leeches, woolly buggers for rainbows.

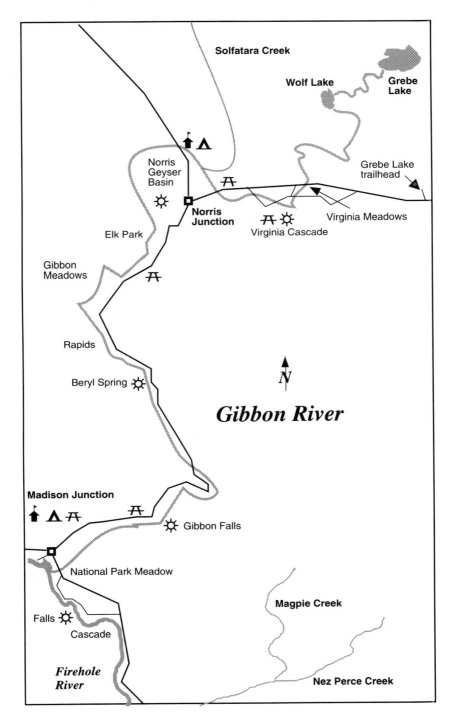

Solfatara Creek

Wolf Lake

Grebe Lake

Norris Geyser Basin

Grebe Lake trailhead

Norris Junction

Virginia Meadows

Virginia Cascade

Elk Park

Gibbon Meadows

Rapids

Beryl Spring

N

Gibbon River

Madison Junction

Gibbon Falls

National Park Meadow

Magpie Creek

Falls

Cascade

Firehole River

Nez Perce Creek

Firehole River

BEST FEATURES: Firehole is ultimate challenge in park for technical fishing for smart fish. Meander through Midway Geyser Basin is the most exotic trout stream in Lower 48; an unworldly experience among cold water fisheries, but be cautious, stay on paths in thermal areas. Abundant wildlife.

SEASON: Saturday, Memorial Day weekend until Loop Road closed.

REGULATIONS: Fly fishing only; rainbow, catch and release; 2 brown trout under 13 inches; 5 brook trout; Old Faithful to Biscuit Basin, closed.

TROUT: Small brook trout, a few small browns above Upper Geyser Basin; rainbows and browns average 12 inches, good chance for 18- to 20-inchers, through Midway Geyser Basin; Madison River's brown spawning run extends into canyon in late fall; larger trout run up Little Firehole, Iron Spring, Nez Perce creeks in mid-summer when water temperatures high.

MILES: 35 miles. Madison Lake to bottom of Upper Geyser Basin, about 15 miles; upper basin to Nez Perce Creek, about 15 miles; lower river "Broads" and canyon, about 5 miles.

CHARACTER: Source is Madison Lake on north slope of Continental Divide above Old Faithful; small mountain stream until it picks up flows of Upper Geyser Basin, Little Firehole, Iron Spring Creek. River drops through riffle-filled run into broader, meandering flows of Biscuit Basin and continues to twist and turn through Midway Geyser Basin and behind Fountain Paint Pot Flats to Nez Perce Creek; classic meadow stream waters with occasional shallow riffles, numerous cutbanks, pools and long glides.Below Nez Perce, pace quickens through the Broads, a string of riffles and swift rocky runs above cascade-falls in canyon and gallop to Madison Junction.

FLOWS: Spring runoff not a major factor; relatively moderate and stable, except in drought years. Watch out for occasional trenches in bed rock bottom and deceptive depths of deeper runs through weed-filled channels.

ACCESS: Madison-Old Faithful road skirts east bank of river with ample pullouts. Side road at Nez Perce Creek leads to Goose Lake and hike-ins on upper west bank; road closed in spring if grizzly bears present. Be wary of bison in Biscuit Basin, Goose Lake area and Fountain Paint Pot Flats.

HATCHES: Tiny flies for scholarly fish sums it up; best fishing in June and early July, and September and October, especially during inclement weather. Baetis and midges in spring and late fall; PMD, caddis, June through September; ants, beetles, hoppers, mid-July through September. Sporadic stone fly and golden stone hatches in canyon in late-June.

FLIES: BWO, blue dun, PMD, Adams, light Cahill, midges,16-22; elk hair caddis, humpies, stimulators, renegades,Wulffs, 12-20; ants, 14-20; beetles, 12-18; hoppers, 8-14. Hare's ear, prince, pheasant tail, soft-hackle nymphs (including beadheads), mayfly and caddis emergers, 14-20; larger nymphs, muddlers, streamers, wooly buggers in fall for browns in canyon.

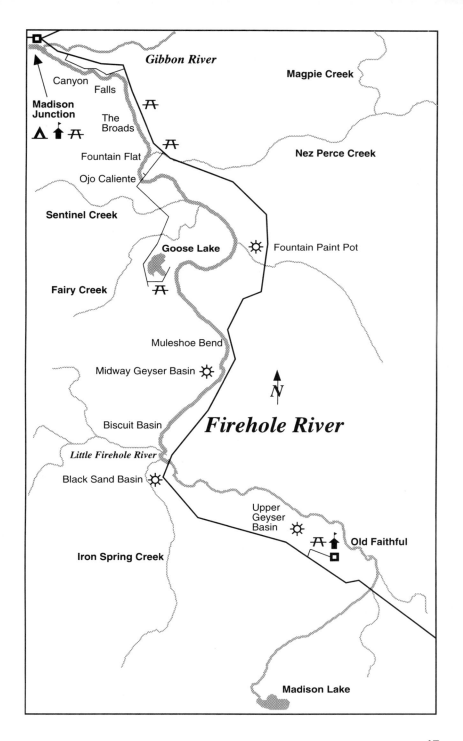

Gibbon River

Magpie Creek

Canyon
Falls

Madison
Junction

The
Broads

Nez Perce Creek

Fountain Flat

Ojo Caliente

Sentinel Creek

Goose Lake

Fountain Paint Pot

Fairy Creek

Muleshoe Bend

Midway Geyser Basin

N

Biscuit Basin

Firehole River

Little Firehole River

Black Sand Basin

Upper
Geyser
Basin

Old Faithful

Iron Spring Creek

Madison Lake

Yellowstone River

BEST FEATURES: The nine miles of river below lake is unique phenomenon in realm of fly fishing for trout. Cutthroat can be kind to exasperatingly selective. Opening Day is a circus; fish elsewhere and return later to appreciate ultimate experience of this stretch. Excellent fishing in canyon waters at Tower Falls and accessible stretches in Black Canyon.

SEASONS: Canyons open Memorial Day weekend; above falls, July 15.

REGULATIONS: Cutthroat catch and release. Closed to fishing: lake outlet to mile below Fishing Bridge, Mud Volcano/Sulphur Cauldron to Alum Creek, and Chittenden Bridge to Inspiration Point (Silver Cord Cascade).

TROUT: Cutthroat in 14- to 24-inch class, lake outlet to Buffalo Ford; 10 to 20 inches in canyons. A few rainbows, cuttbow hybrids below Tower Creek; browns and more rainbows present below Knowles Falls in Black Canyon.

MILES: Lake outlet to Sulphur Cauldron, 10.5 miles; to Alum Creek, 6 miles; to Chittenden Bridge, 2 miles; Grand Canyon about 15 miles; Black Canyon (Roosevelt/Tower Junction bridge to Gardiner) about 20 miles.

CHARACTER: Below lake, river is broad strong-flowing stream with one major rapids (Le Hardy), intermittent swift runs, shallows and riffles, cutbank channels and pools. Easy wading but difficult to cross river above and below Buffalo Ford. Below Alum Creek, stay away from half mile above falls. Canyon waters gallop down deep powerful runs, cascades, pocket waters; many high, rocky outcrops. Fishing is restricted to banks, few side channels, low-water rock gardens. Wading is hazardous in canyons; do not wear waders.

FLOWS: Most years upper river is at prime by Opening Day; autumn flows in drought years can be very low. Spring runoff in Black Canyon can extend into July; summer storms may turn waters off-color below Lamar River.

ACCESS: Loop road hugs river above falls to lake. Best access to lower Grand Canyon is at Tower Falls. Easiest access to Black Canyon is on both sides of Roosevelt/Tower Junction bridge. On Mammoth to Roosevelt Road use trail heads to Hellroaring Creek and Blacktail. Lower canyon, north bank access is above Gardiner. Suspension bridges cross the river on the Blacktail and Hellroaring Creek trails. Take good map; carry water.

HATCHES: Canyon: Stone fly, late-June into July; golden stones, small stone flies can extend through August; caddis, all season; hoppers, late-July, August. Upper River: Stone fly, golden stones, caddis best through July; PMD, BWO, July, August; green drake, July; grasshoppers, July, August; Callibaetis, August; gray drake, September; BWO, midges, late-fall.

FLIES: Stone fly, golden stones, 12-4; caddis, willow fly, humpies, stimulators, 10-18; BW0, PMD, midges, 16-20; light Cahill, Adams, Pink Lady, Wulffs,14-18; drakes, 10-12; grasshoppers, 14-8. Hare's ear, prince, soft-hackle, pheasant tail nymphs, caddis emergers,10-14; black stone and golden stone nymphs, rubber-legs, woolly buggers, muddlers,10-4.

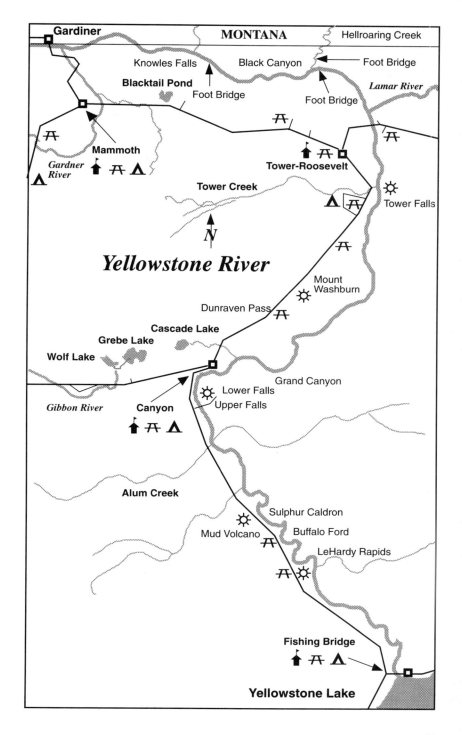

Gardiner

MONTANA

Hellroaring Creek

Knowles Falls

Black Canyon

Foot Bridge

Blacktail Pond

Foot Bridge

Foot Bridge

Lamar River

Mammoth

Tower-Roosevelt

Gardner River

Tower Creek

Tower Falls

N

Yellowstone River

Mount Washburn

Dunraven Pass

Cascade Lake

Grebe Lake

Wolf Lake

Grand Canyon

Gibbon River

Canyon

Lower Falls

Upper Falls

Alum Creek

Sulphur Caldron

Mud Volcano

Buffalo Ford

LeHardy Rapids

Fishing Bridge

Yellowstone Lake

Upper Yellowstone, Snake, Lewis

BEST FEATURES: The epitome of wilderness solitude, a trek to the birth of the Yellowstone or Snake is as far from a road as you can get in the Lower 48. Both flow off the Continental Divide south of park. Upper Yellowstone and Thorofare Creek equal a life-time adventure. At Two Ocean Pass, a spring-fed trickle forks to become Atlantic and Pacific creeks.

SEASONS: All rivers, streams in Yellowstone drainage above falls open July 15; lakes in drainage, including Yellowstone, open June 15. Streams and lakes of Snake drainage open Saturday of Memorial Day weekend.

REGULATIONS: Cutthroat catch and release, except Yellowstone Lake and tributaries, 2 under 13 inches; brown trout, 2, except Lewis Falls to canyon, catch and release; lake trout, 2 in lewis and Shoshone lakes; must kill lake trout in Yellowstone and Heart lakes; brook trout, 5. (Wyoming's Teton Wilderness opens May 21; 2 fish, only 1 over 20 inches. See Page 54.)

TROUT: Yellowstone River: cutthroat, 14 to 24 inches. Snake River: cutthroat and browns in 10- to 16-inch class. Lewis Channel: browns, 14 to 24 inches in autumn. Lewis River: browns average 12 inches, a few surprises.

MILES: Upper Yellowstone meanders about 20 miles to park's south border, another 30 to delta . Snake flows 42 miles from source just south of park's boundary to confluence with Lewis. Lewis is approximately 20 miles, includes 4-mile channel between Lewis and Shoshone lakes, 2-mile outlet to Lewis Falls, 4-mile upper meadows and 10-mile canyon.

CHARACTER: Yellowstone gallops down slopes of Yount's Peak to marshy flats of ancient Yellowstone Lake, meanders in meadow stream fashion — glides, pools, riffles, runs — to delta. Snake cuts through heavily eroded valley in strings of riffles, runs, pocket waters and pools; numerous side channels and gravel bars. Lewis best in channel between lakes, Lewis Lake outlet, falls plunge pool, and upper meadow; canyon inaccessible.

FLOWS: Yellowstone runoff peaks in late-June. Snake moderates by July; fall flows low in drought years. Lewis runoff flows determined by lake.

ACCESS: Get back country permit to camp at ranger stations. Best times late-summer, early fall; some areas closed in spring to protect grizzly bears, which are present all season. Hike in groups of 3 or more; keep clean camp. Area is mosquito-infested spring through mid-summer. Yellowstone delta is best reached via boat to east bank of Southeast Arm and long hike. Top half of river is best reached by guided horse trip via trails west of Cody or north of Jackson. Snake River-South Boundary trail terrain rises and falls; take Heart Lake fork to reach lower Yellowstone, or continue east over divide to upper river. Consult USGS topographical or commercial trail maps.

HATCHES: Watch for PMDs, BWOs, green drakes, caddis, willow flies.

FLIES: PMD, BWO, Adams, light Cahill, elk hair caddis, humpies, stimulators, Wulffs, renegades,12-18. Grasshoppers, 8-14. Hare's ear, prince, pheasant tail, soft-hackle nymphs, caddis larva and emergers,10-16.

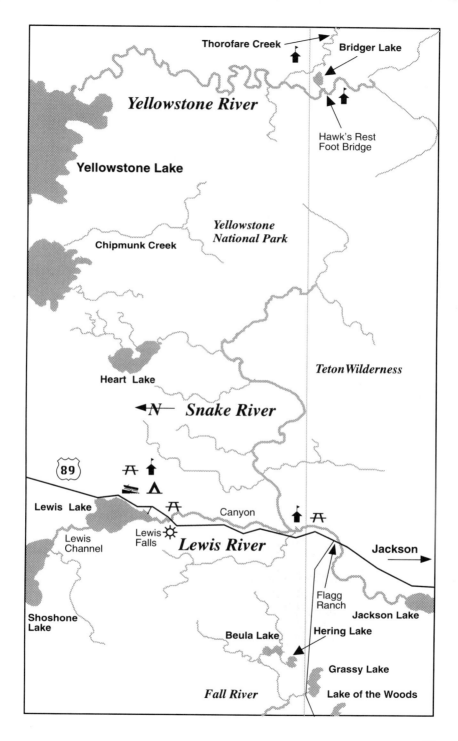

21

Lamar River and Slough Creek

BEST FEATURES: Lamar's vivacious cutthroat rank it amidst West's premier streams. Slough Creek's charm haunts the dreams of all fly fishers.

SEASONS: Saturday, Memorial Day weekend through October 31.

REGULATIONS: Cutthroat catch and release; 2 rainbow, 5 brook trout.

TROUT: Lamar's cutthroat below Soda Butte Creek mostly in 15-inch range but anticipate fish 18 to 24 inches, also a few rainbows and hybrids; upper Lamar's cutthroat in 10- to 18-inch range. Slough Creek harbors strong population of 16-inch cutthroat, with good number 18 to 24 inches.

(Volunteer Angler Report card filled out by former President Jimmy Carter following three days in August 1993 on Slough Creek: 4 cutthroat 10-12", 2 CT 12-14", 3 CT 14-16", 7 CT 14-16", 8 CT 18-20" and 1 CT over 20".)

MILES: Lamar flows about 55 miles from headwaters to Yellowstone. Upper 30 miles are above Soda Butte Creek; lower stretch almost equally divided between valley run and canyon. Slough Creek flows 16 miles in park to join Lamar; three meadow runs range from 2 to 4 miles in length.

CHARACTER: Lamar tumbles in swift runs down a descent of almost 3,000 feet from western slopes of Absarokas to top of Lamar Valley southeast of Soda Butte. Valley run is through broad, sometimes marshy floodplain, marked by serpentine turns through eroded glacial till, long riffles and runs and shallow pools. Top two miles of canyon fast-paced, filled with large boulders, cascades and pocket waters; canyon run flattens a little above merger with Slough Creek before final plunge to Yellowstone. The many meanders of Slough Creek's meadow runs are marked by numerous cutbanks and pools, long glides, riffles and side channels. Lower meadow and middle meadow divided by steep cascading canyon; upper two meadows divided by wooded tumbling run filled with rocky riffles, pocket waters.

FLOWS: Spring surge on Lamar starts to drop by July but river can rise dramatically all season from muddy runoff of summer storms. Slough Creek subsides by late-June or July, continues to drop through summer and fall.

ACCESS: Lamar Valley and top of canyon paralleled by road; lower canyon difficult to wade. Slough Creek's first meadow reached from road or campground. Start from trailhead parking lot, not campground, to reach second meadow, a 2.5-mile hike; third meadow is another 6 miles.

HATCHES: Stone fly, late-June, early July; golden stones, July-August; caddis, PMD, Baetis, all season; green drake, July; Trichos, August; hoppers, beetles, July – September; gray drake, September; BWO, late-fall.

FLIES: Stone flies, 4-6; golden stone, 6-8; elk hair caddis, humpies, stimulators, 12-18; PMD, BWO, olive or tan parachute hare's ear, 14-20; light Cahill, Adams, Pink Lady, Wulffs, 12-18; Trichos, 22-24; beetles, 14-18; hoppers, 8-14. Dark stones, woolly buggers, rubber-legs, 2-10; hare's ear, pheasant tail, soft-hackle nymphs, Zug bug, caddis emergers, 12-16.

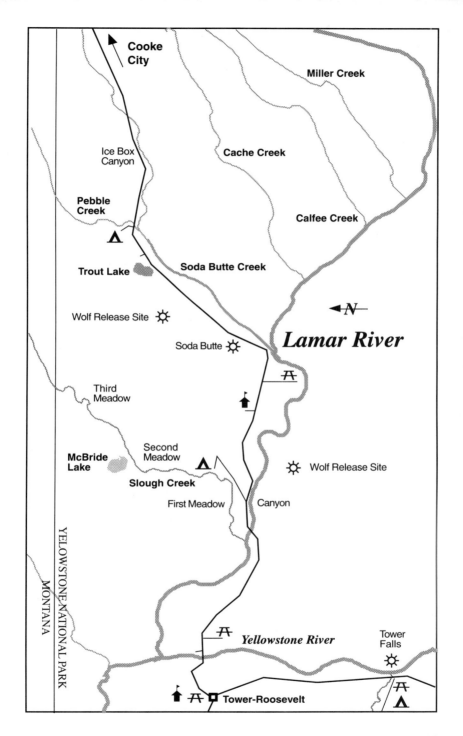

Cooke City

Miller Creek

Ice Box Canyon

Cache Creek

Pebble Creek

Calfee Creek

⛺

Trout Lake

Soda Butte Creek

Wolf Release Site ☼

N

Soda Butte ☼

Lamar River

Third Meadow

🏕

Second Meadow

McBride Lake

Λ

☼ Wolf Release Site

Slough Creek

First Meadow

Canyon

YELOWSTONE NATIONAL PARK

MONTANA

🏕

Yellowstone River

Tower Falls

☼

🏕 🏕 □ Tower-Roosevelt

🏕
Λ

Bechler River, upper Fall River

BEST FEATURES: Bechler Meadow's brawny trout tender spring creek challenges in secluded backcountry niche of park. Fall plunges over four of Cascade Corner's 21 waterfalls. Rare whooping crane sighting is possible.

SEASON: Saturday, Memorial Day weekend through October 31.

REGULATIONS: Cutthroat and rainbows, catch and release.

TROUT: Rainbows out number cutthroat in lower sections of both rivers; native cutthroat reign above falls. Bechler Meadow holds strong population of 16- to 18-inch trout, with fair number in 5-pound range. Mostly moderate-sized cutthroat in upstream pocket waters and tributaries of Bechler and in upper Fall and Beula Lake, its source. Grayling in nearby Horseshoe Lake.

MILES: Fall River flows about 50 miles from Pitchstone Plateau to confluence with Henry's Fork, including about 20 miles in park. Bechler's tributary headwaters are about 20 miles above its merger with Fall at Cave Falls.

CHARACTER: Upper pocket water stretch of Bechler cascades down plateau to canyon and plunges over 100-foot Colonnade Falls. Crystal-clear waters of three-mile meadow below falls meander through marshy flat; final couple miles of river gallop down a lava rock cascade to Fall. Channels in meadow are usually too deep to wade. Fish cautiously as you would on a spring creek; grassy overhangs along banks and deep pools of cutbanks harbor large trout. A suspension bridge crosses river at top end of meadow. Fall meanders across meadows and forest below Beula Lake and then drops dramatically down string of swift cascading runs to scenic Cave Falls.

FLOWS: Spring runoff on Fall usually peaks in late-June but may extend into July. Runoff also often late on Bechler. Both fish best in late-summer.

ACCESS: To reach Bechler Meadows drive east from Ashton, Idaho, on State Highway 47 to Cave Falls Road. Five-mile trail starts from Ranger Station. Backcountry permit required to camp overnight at designated sites. Beula Lake and upper Fall can be reached from Ashton, or park's South Entrance or Jackson, Wyo., via Flagg Ranch-Reclamation Road; trailheads are located at Loon Lake and Grassy Lake. Campgrounds are at Grassy Lake, Cave Falls, Horseshoe Lake and other sites in Targhee National Forest. Meadow marshes of this corner of park are often mosquito-infested into August. Grizzly bear country; hike in groups of 3 or more.

HATCHES: Stone fly, early July, golden stones, late-July, on Fall. Mayfly hatches sporadic, not well recorded. Caddis are plentiful most of season and grasshoppers and beetles are effective in late-summer, autumn.

FLIES: Stone flies, 4-8; golden stones, 6-10; elk hair caddis, stimulators, humpies, 10-18; PMD, BWO, light Cahill, Adams, Wulffs, renegade, 14-20; grasshoppers, 8-14; beetles, 14-18; midges, and mosquito, 16-22. Dark stone, golden stone nymphs, rubber-legs, woolly buggers, muddlers, 4-10; hare's ear, prince, pheasant tail, soft-hackle nymphs, bead-heads, 12-18.

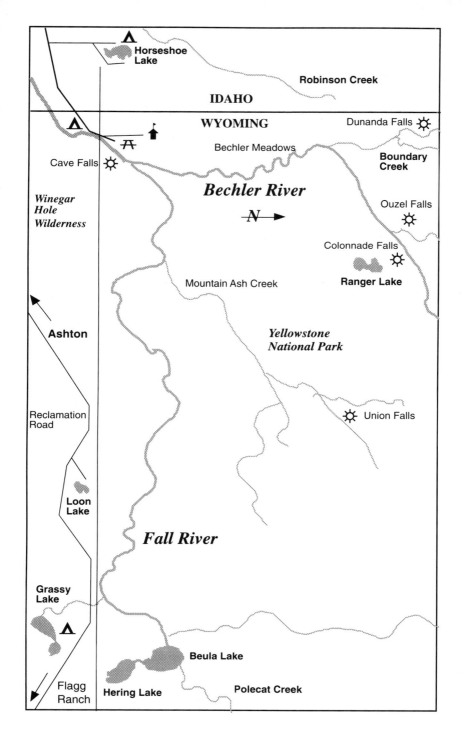

Horseshoe Lake

Robinson Creek

IDAHO

WYOMING

Dunanda Falls ☼

Bechler Meadows

Boundary Creek

Cave Falls ☼

Bechler River

Winegar Hole Wilderness

Ouzel Falls ☼

─*N*→

Colonnade Falls ☼

Mountain Ash Creek

Ranger Lake

Ashton

Yellowstone National Park

Reclamation Road

☼ Union Falls

Loon Lake

Fall River

Grassy Lake

Beula Lake

Flagg Ranch

Hering Lake

Polecat Creek

Stillwater adventures:

Yellowstone Lake and backcountry sanctuarys

Illegal introduction of lake trout into Yellowstone Lake cast a pall over an amazing success story: the recovery of the lake's native Yellowstone cutthroat trout. Biologists now face the grim specter of trying to prevent the predatory non-native fish from destroying a world-renown fishery.

According to park biologists:

■ A small number of lake trout have been in the lake for 10 years or more. The fish may have been introduced over even a longer period of time.

■ Lake trout caught by anglers and biologists in 1994 and 1995 appear to be the first and second age classes of successful reproduction by larger fish. The size of some indicate more are approaching sexual maturity.

This means Yellowstone Lake is on the verge of a rapid increase in its lake trout population. Time may be running out to turn back the tide and ensure the long-term survival of the cutthroat.

"I think everyone agrees that if there's a window of opportunity open for us, it won't stay open very long," says Lynn Kaeding, acting director of Yellowstone fisheries for the U.S. Fish and Wildlife Service.

Park officials are moving aggressively to at least suppress the lake trout, although the great size of the lake may overwhelm attempts to eradicate the predators. Initial efforts are focused on eliminating the larger lake trout. Once they grow 20 inches or more, their consumption skyrockets.

Loss of the lake's cutthroat would have a domino effect on trout populations in the upper Yellowstone River, as well as on other wildlife. They are a major food source for grizzly bears, otters, bald eagles, osprey, cormorants, pelicans, and 36 other birds and mammals. To lose this marvelous fishery would seriously impair the region's fishing, tourism and recreation businesses. There is a $10,000 reward for information leading to arrest and conviction of those who illegally transplanted the lake trout.

Yellowstone Lake anglers are required to kill all lake trout they net. The fish can be kept but anglers are asked to take them to a ranger station or visitors center for inspection by a biologist. In 1996, the mandatory kill requirement of lake trout was extended to Heart Lake in an attempt to save its cutthroat, a subspecies of the Snake River finespotted cutthroat.

The 136-square mile Yellowstone Lake, which opens to fishing June 15, is the most popular fishery in the park. More than 50,000 anglers a year or about 40 percent of the park's anglers ply its waters. And even after a 100-year history of over fishing, including commercial fishing, it still supports the largest inland cutthroat population in North America.

A 14-inch minimum catch size imposed in 1970 helped curb the intense over fishing of the 1950s and '60s, but the rising fishing pressure continued to eliminate older, large cutthroat from the lake. The two-fish under 13 inches limit imposed in 1973 was designed to improve the population age structure and gain an increased number of older, large trout. It was hoped this would provide a population stability and productivity that would more closely resemble historic cutthroat populations. It worked.

A gill-net survey by Fish and Wildlife showed the lake's cutthroat size structure may be approaching equilibrium, with an average size of 15 inches. Anglers report 24 percent of landed trout exceed 16 inches. Catch rate is .8 fish per hour from shore; 1.4 per hour from a boat. "Currently five large trout (14-18 inches) are captured and released for each trout under (13 inches) creeled," states a Fish and Wildlife report. "Over two-thirds of all anglers catch one or more trout, and one-third creel one or more. Excellent landing rates, often associated with 'no kill' regulations ... have been sustained (with the) privilege of harvesting trout for a campfire meal."

The lake's 7,770-foot elevation means ice-out occurs in late-May or early June. Best action is sight casting to cruising fish. Boaters do better, but should be wary of high winds, intense storms. Waders along shoreline find fishing improves by early July as lake warms. Cutthroat cruise shores in 4 to 10 feet of water along sandbars and near points and inlets; generally, best areas are shallow bays in fingers of lake. Wet fly patterns include stone fly nymphs, damsel fly, green and black woolly buggers, sculpins, streamers, leeches, scuds and beadhead nymphs. Present dry flies on long leaders. Try elk hair caddis, terrestrial or attractor patterns, and give them an occasional twitch. Minor mayfly hatches include Callibaetis, Baetis, Tricho.

Other exemplary lakes in the park include:

Lewis Lake — A 2,716-acre lake on South Entrance road; large lake trout and browns, some brook trout in tributaries; best in spring and late-fall. Due to sudden high winds, canoers should stick to shorelines, even to get to popular Lewis River channel and Shoshone Lake. Channel is principal spawning stream for browns in late-fall, which also congregate at outlet.

Shoshone Lake — An 8,050-acre lake upstream from Lewis Lake; large lake trout and browns, some good-sized brook trout; best in spring to late-summer. Canoers, float-tubers should be wary of sudden, intense storms.

Heart Lake — A 2,150-acre backcountry lake in the Snake River drainage, about 8 miles northeast of Lewis Lake; large cutthroat and lake trout; best in spring and late-fall. Grizzly bear country; hike in groups of 3 or more.

Grebe Lake — A 156-acre lake, source of Gibbon River; 3.5-mile hike from Norris-Canyon road; moderate-sized rainbows and grayling; both in nearby Wolf Lake, too; best in mid-summer. Grizzly bear country; don't hike alone.

Beula Lake — A 107- acre lake, source of Fall River; 2.5 mile hike from Grassy Lake inlet, reached via the Flagg Ranch Road (Reclamation Road) from Ashton or the South Entrance; moderate-sized cutthroat; best in midsummer, fall. Also good fishing in nearby Hering Lake and upper Fall River.

Eastern Idaho

Treasure trove of cutthroat and rainbow streams

Eastern Idaho's stellar wild trout streams and a peerless trophy trout lake promise fly fishers a piscatorial smorgasbord to feed eternal memories.

Superb fisheries for cutthroat, the Native Sons of the Intermountain West, are found in the South Fork of the Snake, Teton and Fall rivers and Henry's Lake. Perhaps the most esteemed trout of the region are challenging rainbows of Railroad Ranch and Box Canyon fame in the Henry's Fork of the Snake. But they reside in only two short stretches of this astounding river filled with trophy fish from Island Park to St. Anthony.

A champion dry fly stream, the South Fork is the region's best example of wild trout management proving the benefits of strict regulations. In addition to robust populations of Yellowstone cutthroat and Snake River finespotted cutthroat, it is Idaho's record-setting waters for brown trout. At the top of the drainage, Henry's Lake harbors trophy cutthroat and rainbow-cutthroat hybrids, and is Idaho's record-setter for brook trout. Basking in their shadows of fame are the often overlooked but exemplary Fall and Teton rivers. The Fall flows out of the little-explored southwest corner of Yellowstone National Park. The Teton flows through a pastoral valley past the western slopes of the majestic Teton Mountains and plunges into a deep, remote canyon to join the Henry's Fork. A hidden gem on-the-rebound, just south of the Greater Yellowstone Ecosystem, is the upper Blackfoot River. It is a side-trip worth pursuing, along with many others.

Except for the Teton's canyon, public access to fish Idaho's Upper Snake River drainage is excellent. Large tracts of federal and state lands make it one of the best natural playgrounds in the West. Foremost in this equation is Targhee National Forest that straddles the Idaho-Wyoming border. An excellent federal map details forest roads, campgrounds and trail heads in the Island Park, Ashton, Teton and Palisades ranger districts. Obtain one at any of the Ranger District offices or the Eastern Idaho Visitors Center and use it to explore other worthy fishing opportunities in the region.

For starters, consider these suggestions:

A tributary of the Henry's Fork, the Buffalo River is a beautiful little stream fly fishers of all ages and skills can enjoy. Its gentle, spring-fed flows glide past Island Park's largest campground on its north bank. It is stocked with hatchery rainbows, and has a good population of small wild brook trout. Idaho offers a six-fish bag limit for hatchery rainbows and permits a 10-fish bonus on brookies.

The Warm River, which joins the Henry's Fork downstream from Mesa Falls 10 miles west of Ashton, is another small stream popular with families. Hatchery rainbows are planted in the campground area, and it is a spawning stream for brown trout that come up out of the Henry's Fork. Mostly brook trout are found above Warm River Springs.

Fly fishers en route to Bechler Meadows, or the scenic Cave Falls on the Fall River in the southwest corner of Yellowstone, can make a side trip to an isolated crystal clear lake with a rare population of grayling. Horseshoe Lake is just west of the park boundary, seven miles north of Cave Falls road. Rainbows also await float-tubers or canoe anglers.

The same road provides access to Robinson Creek, a tributary of Warm River, that flows through a deep, wooded canyon. This classic mountain stream holds the promise of a four-species day. Anglers have a shot at netting cutthroat, rainbows, browns and whitefish.

Fishing these tributary waters is a fairly straight-forward proposition with standard caddis, mayfly and attractor patterns. Backcountry trout are often less wary than those pursued so heavily on better known streams.

An irrigation impoundment on the Henry's Fork, Island Park Reservoir is in a recovery stage. In 1992, at the height of the recent drought, it was drawn down to the original stream bed. Idaho Fish and Game took advantage of the drawdown to poison non-game fish like chubs and suckers. It was restocked with rainbows, rainbow-cutthroat hybrids, Lahontan cutthroats and kokanee salmon, and is beginning to make a strong comeback. Float-tubers and shoreline fly casters favor the coves and points that line the Grizzly Springs and Fingers areas of Island Park Reservoir near the West End Campground, west of Harriman State Park. It fishes best in early spring or late-fall.

Palisades Reservoir on the Idaho-Wyoming state line controls the flows of the South Fork of the Snake. The reservoir is basically a deep-water fishery and gets little attention from fly fishers. It contains good-sized finespotted Snake River cutthroat, brown and lake trout, as well as kokanee salmon.

Several of its tributaries are attractive alternatives for fly fishers who like to fish small mountain streams. Most popular are Big Elk, McCoy and Bear creeks for excellent cutthroat fishing. The Salt River, a Wyoming tributary, draws fly fishers in late-fall when heavy drawdown of the reservoir exposes the river channel on the Idaho side of the state line. Their goal is to intercept brown trout running upstream to spawn.

Downstream from Palisades Dam are two major cutthroat spawning tributaries of the South Fork, Rainey and Pine creeks. An alpine side trip to the Upper Palisades Lakes on the headwaters of Palisades Creek also promises accommodating cutthroat.

For more details on eastern Idaho's fisheries and matchless other top-notch options in the state, obtain "Fly Fisher's Guide to Idaho" by Ken Retallic and Rocky Barker.

Henry's Fork of the Snake River

BEST FEATURES: World famous trout stream with large rainbows, profuse and varied aquatic fly hatches. Spectacular scenery, abundant wildlife.

SEASONS: Upper river north of Vernon Bridge, Memorial Day weekend though Nov. 30; Harriman State Park, June 15 to Nov. 30; Harriman Bird Sanctuary, June 15 to Sept. 30. Below Vernon Bridge, open all year.

REGULATIONS: Henry's Lake Outlet to Island Park Dam, 6-trout limit; Box Canyon to Riverside Campground, catch and release (Harriman State Park, fly fishing only); Riverside to St. Anthony, 2-trout limit, none between 8 and 16 inches; St. Anthony to mouth, 6-trout limit.

TROUT: Upper river, rainbows, some over 25 inches; a few cutthroat and brook trout. Below Mesa Falls, rainbows and cutthroat-rainbow hybrids, both able to exceed 24 inches; growing number of large brown trout.

MILES: Mile 0: Henry's Lake Outlet; Mile 12: Big Springs confluence; Mile 16: Macks Inn; Mile 20: Coffee Pot Rapids; Mile 25: Island Park Dam (Box Canyon); Mile 28: Last Chance; Mile 30: Harriman State Park; Mile 35: Osborne Bridge; Mile 41: Riverside Campground; Mile 50: Upper Mesa Falls; Mile 60: Warm River confluence; Mile 71: Ashton Dam; Mile 77, Fall River confluence (Chester Dam); Mile 90: St. Anthony; Mile 100: Teton River confluence; Mile 120: Joins South Fork to form Snake River.

CHARACTER: Gentle meadow stream from Outlet to Coffee Pot Rapids. Box Canyon strewn with boulders, large cobble stones. Last Chance to Riverside has broad, flat meandering glides, few riffles. Riverside to Warm River, river plunges through Cardiac Canyon, heavy pocket waters, three waterfalls. Below Warm River, long, deep glides, riffles and pocket waters. Ashton Dam to St. Anthony, long, wide glides, shallow pools and riffles.

FLOWS: Average flows are 400 cubic feet per second to 1,500 cfs, with higher irrigation flows in mid-July and August. Dams help curb spring runoff.

ACCESS: All public land on upper river in Targhee National Forest, except for resorts, developments. Highway signs mark access sites north of St. Anthony. Many boat ramps for float boats and canoes; no motors. Difficult wading in canyons. Falls make middle of Cardiac Canyon inaccessible.

HATCHES: Stone fly, late-May and June; golden stones and willow flies June to July. Caddis, April through June below Ashton, June and early July in Island Park. Green drake, mid-June below Ashton, late-June in Island Park. Small green drake or Flav, July in Island Park. Pale morning dun, May to mid-July below Ashton, June and July in Island Park. Baetis, early-spring, mid-summer, late-fall. Tricos and Callibaetis, mid-summer. Mahogany dun, September in Island Park. Gray drake, September below Ashton. Midges, late-fall, winter, early-spring below Ashton.

FLIES: Stoneflies, 4-6; golden stone, 8-14. Drakes, 10-12. Elk hair caddis, humpies, stimulators, Wulffs, renegades, 12 -18. Mayflies, 16-22. Nymphs, emergers in similar sizes. Beadheads, San Juan worms in winter.

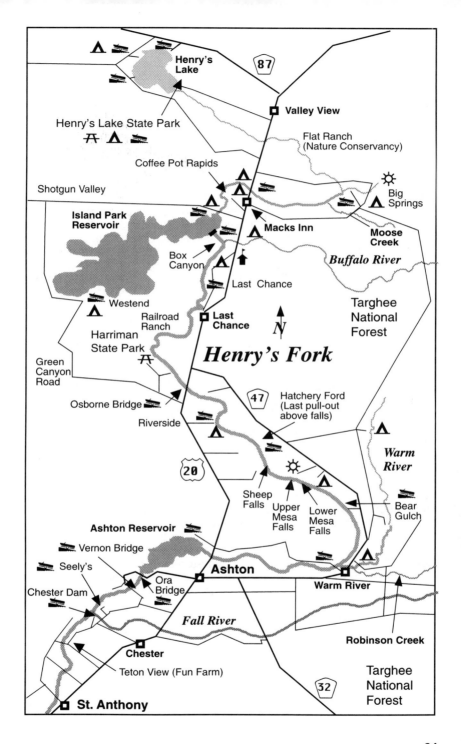

Henry's Lake

87

Valley View

Henry's Lake State Park

Flat Ranch
(Nature Conservancy)

Coffee Pot Rapids

Shotgun Valley

Big Springs

Island Park
Reservoir

Macks Inn

Moose Creek

Box Canyon

Buffalo River

Last Chance

Westend

Targhee National Forest

Railroad Ranch

Last Chance

Harriman State Park

N

Green Canyon Road

Henry's Fork

Osborne Bridge

47

Hatchery Ford
(Last pull-out above falls)

Riverside

20

Warm River

Sheep Falls

Upper Mesa Falls

Lower Mesa Falls

Bear Gulch

Ashton Reservoir

Vernon Bridge

Seely's

Ashton

Chester Dam

Ora Bridge

Warm River

Fall River

Robinson Creek

Chester

Teton View (Fun Farm)

32

Targhee National Forest

St. Anthony

Henry's Lake

BEST FEATURES: Premier trophy trout lake, perhaps best in the Lower 48 states. Spectacular mountain scenery. Bald eagles common.

SEASONS: Henry's Lake — Saturday of Memorial Day weekend to Oct. 31, between hours of 5 a.m. and 9 p.m. daily. Tributary creeks — Aug. 1 to Aug. 31; except Hatchery Creek, closed to fishing.

REGULATIONS: Two-fish limit; brook trout must be counted in bag and possession limit on lake and in tributaries. Must quit fishing if 2 trout taken in possession. Posted boundaries at Staley's Spring and mouth of Hatchery Creek closed to fishing.

TROUT: Yellowstone cutthroat, cutthroat-rainbow hybrids and brook trout. Average mean size for hybrids is 19 inches and 16 inches for cutthroat and brook trout. Potential for trophy fish with all three species, exceeding 30 inches for hybrids, 25 inches for cutthroat and 20 inches for brook trout. Brook trout record — 7 lbs. 1 oz., 23.5 inches — in 1978.

SIZE: 6,500 acres, 4 miles wide and 5 miles long; average depth of 12 feet, deepest point about 25 feet. Irrigation dam regulates water depth.

CHARACTER: Sits at 6,470 feet of elevation in bowl at base of Centennial Mountains on the Continental Divide. Can experience violent storms and high winds, which cause heavy wave action. Float-tubers should take care to not overextend themselves. Lake is fed by numerous creeks and springs. Summer vegetation growth often makes fishing difficult; fish channels between aquatic plants and spring-fed holes in lake.

ACCESS: Very limited opportunities for wading, except north shore in vicinity of state hatchery. The lake is best fished from boats or float tubes. State Highway 87 skirts north end of lake. Gravel forest road, No. 055, skirts west shore; Red Rock Lakes Road, forest road No. 053, skirts south shore. Most of lake is surrounded by private land. Locations to launch boats or float tubes are about equally divided between public access sites and commercial resorts. Latter, and state park, charge a fee.

HATCHES: Dry flies are very minor players. Virtually all the action is with wet flies on full sinking lines or sinking tips. Damsel fly hatch, the only real one on the lake, is in late-June to mid-July, but it is still fished as a wet fly. Scuds, or fresh water shrimp, leeches and nymphs are in the lake year-round. Streamer patterns are especially effective in fall for brook trout.

FLIES: Scuds, damsel fly nymphs, leeches, woolly buggers, crystal buggers and Henry's Lake renegade. Streamer patterns for dace and sculpin and long slender ones for leeches. Leeches, in brown, light olive or Canadian red, perform best in 4-6. Green or olive scuds and damsel nymphs, 8-12. Woolly buggers, crystal buggers and streamers, 8-10, in red, Canadian red, black, purple, orange, olive and brown, as well as the Halloween series of variegated colors. Muddlers and streamers, 2-8.

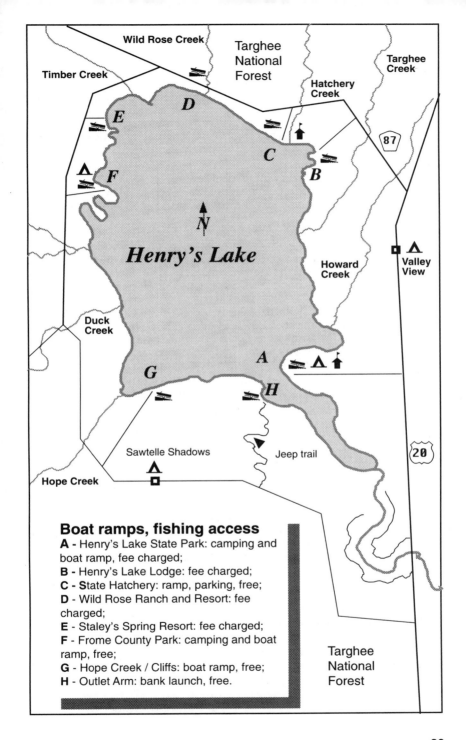

Boat ramps, fishing access

A - Henry's Lake State Park: camping and boat ramp, fee charged;

B - Henry's Lake Lodge: fee charged;

C - State Hatchery: ramp, parking, free;

D - Wild Rose Ranch and Resort: fee charged;

E - Staley's Spring Resort: fee charged;

F - Frome County Park: camping and boat ramp, free;

G - Hope Creek / Cliffs: boat ramp, free;

H - Outlet Arm: bank launch, free.

Fall River

BEST FEATURES: Often overlooked classic mountain stream that offers prime opportunities for solitary fishing in national forest west of Cave Falls. Lower river a few miles above mouth is good family fishing outing.

SEASON: Saturday of Memorial Day weekend through Nov. 30.

REGULATIONS: Managed as a wild trout fishery, 2-trout bag limit in Idaho. Need permit in park; cutthroat, catch-and-release; rainbow, two-fish limit.

TROUT: Upper river holds cutthroat, a few rainbows; lower river holds mostly rainbows and a few cutthroat-rainbow hybrids. Majority are in the 9- to 15-inch range; a few exceed 20 inches, especially in the lower reaches.

MILES: 52 miles from its headwaters on the Pitchstone Plateau in park to its confluence with the Henry's Fork. Mile 18: park boundary; Mile 22: Sheep Falls; Mile 27: Targhee National Forest boundary; Mile 35: Kirkham Bridge; Mile 40: Highway 32 bridge; Mile 44: low-head diversion dam; Mile 50: U.S. 20 bridge; Mile 52: Chester Reservoir on Henry's Fork.

CHARACTER: Drops average rate of 50 feet per mile from altitude of 8,500 feet at headwaters to 5,030 feet at mouth. Canyon is often deep, picturesque. Main waterfalls are Cave Falls just inside park and Sheep Falls 4 miles downstream. Numerous cascades and rapids in upper reaches. Canyon begins to widen and river flattens out some below State Highway 32. Above and below U.S. 20 river runs through heavily eroded lava rock chutes. Difficult to wade in upper reaches due to slippery cobble stones. Cannot be floated above State Highway 32.

FLOWS: Averages 730 cubic feet per second after high, muddy spring runoff. Irrigation diversions can almost dry up lower river in drought years. Summer flows remain steady above Targhee Forest boundary.

ACCESS: Take State Highway 47 east from Ashton to reach Cave Falls area in park, or turn south at Marysville to reach Reclamation Road that goes to Flagg Ranch in Wyoming. A few national forest roads lead to canyon rim in Idaho, where you have to bushwhack into canyon. Downstream most access points are at bridge crossings. Only boat ramp is at State Highway 32 bridge. Pull-out is at mouth, above Chester Dam on the Henry's Fork. Good gravel road follows south bank upstream from U.S. 20; turn east at Fall River General Store, drive about 5 miles to reach river access sites.

HATCHES: Mayfly and caddis hatches aren't dated well, but it has them all. Excellent stonefly hatch in late-June, although water often high. Grasshoppers good in late-summer. Strong Baetis, BWO, hatch in fall.

FLIES: Stone fly dry flies, 4-6, and golden stones, 6-10 ; nymphs, woolly buggers and rubber-legs, 4-14. Dry flies: PMD, BWO, Adams, light Cahill, elk hair caddis, humpies, stimulators, Wulffs, renegades,12-18. Grasshoppers, 8-14. Hare's ear nymph, prince, pheasant tail, caddis emergers,10-16. Also beadheads in same sizes. Streamer patterns, 2-8, good in fall.

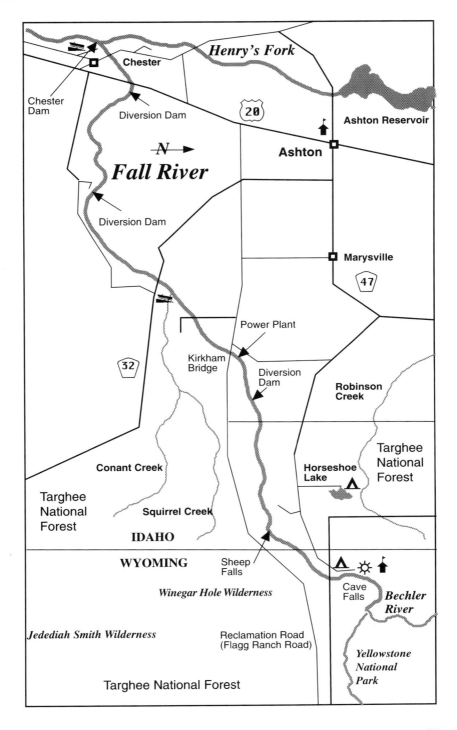

Chester

Henry's Fork

Chester Dam

Diversion Dam

(20)

Ashton Reservoir

N

Fall River

Ashton

Diversion Dam

Marysville

(47)

Power Plant

(32)

Kirkham Bridge

Diversion Dam

Robinson Creek

Conant Creek

Horseshoe Lake

Targhee National Forest

Targhee National Forest

Squirrel Creek

IDAHO

WYOMING

Sheep Falls

Cave Falls

Bechler River

Winegar Hole Wilderness

Jedediah Smith Wilderness

Reclamation Road (Flagg Ranch Road)

Yellowstone National Park

Targhee National Forest

Teton River

BEST FEATURES: Upper river flows through scenic valley with grand views of Tetons, abundant wildlife. Remote canyon, deep and picturesque.

SEASON: Saturday, Memorial Day weekend through Nov. 30; except Teton Creek and its tributaries, which is July 1 to Nov. 30.

REGULATIONS: Two-fish limit on cutthroat trout, none between 8 and 16 inches; 6-fish limit on rainbows; 10 brook trout bonus.

TROUT: Cutthroat in 10- to 15-inch class, growing number over 18 inches in valley; some to 24 inches in canyon. Wild rainbow and cutthroat-rainbow hybrids up to 26 inches. Hatchery rainbows being phased out.

MILES: About 75 miles from where Trail and Pine creeks join to form Teton to its confluence with the Henry's Fork of the Snake.

CHARACTER: For its first 30 miles, the Teton is a smooth, meandering meadow stream flowing through broad basin dotted by 100-year-old farms and ranches. Its wide, slow flows and glassy glides are fed by numerous tributaries and surrounding marshy riparian areas. Below State Highway 33, the river plunges into a deep, picturesque canyon and gallops downstream for about 30 miles through pocket waters rumbled by huge volcanic rocks. A few miles below Teton Dam, river splits into two 10-mile irrigation canals.

FLOWS: Spring runoff can continue past mid-July in wet year. Summer flows moderate to sometimes very low, depending on irrigation needs.

ACCESS: In upper valley, turn west at public access signs on Highway 33. County road skirts west bank of river with turnoffs leading to west bank sites. Most are at bridges; boat ramps at all but Fox Creek sites. Excellent float fishing; cast to rising fish. Rainey site is largest with most access for waders. Work your way upstream and downstream at others when flows are low. Bottom very silty in some stretches, hard to wade. End valley float at Harrop's Bridge. Canyon waters dangerous. Do not attempt to float between Highway 33 and Spring Hollow. Rough trails down steep cliffs at Badger and Bitch creeks on upper end. At lower end, turn off Highway 33 to failed Teton Dam, turn right on dirt road at parking lot. First left a mile east leads to old boat ramp. Next left into canyon requires 4x4, high clearance. Walk mile or two upstream for better fishing. Beware of rattlesnakes.

HATCHES: Canyon: Stonefly hatch third week of June, followed by golden stonefly hatch. Hoppers and caddis mid-summer into fall; caddis, usual mayflies on slower stretches. Upper Valley: Western green drake late-June; PMD, Baetis, tricos, Callibaetis July through October; hoppers and ants late-July to frost; gray drake, late-August and September.

FLIES: Stoneflies, golden stones, stimulators, 6-10; hoppers, 8-14; green and gray drakes, 10; small mayflies, 16-22; elk hair caddis, stimulators, 12-16; Wulffs, renegades, 10-14. Golden stone nymphs, rubberlegs, woolly buggers, 8-14. Caddis and mayfly nymphs, hare's ear, 12-20.

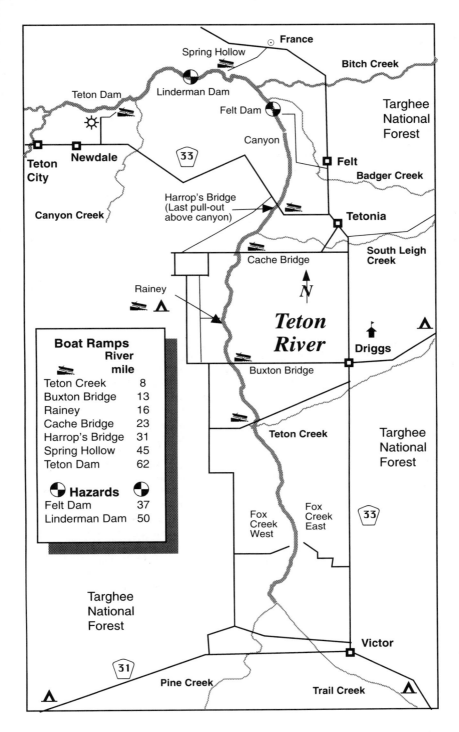

France

Spring Hollow

Bitch Creek

Teton Dam

Linderman Dam

Felt Dam

Canyon

Targhee
National
Forest

Teton
City

Newdale

33

Felt

Badger Creek

Canyon Creek

Harrop's Bridge
(Last pull-out
above canyon)

Tetonia

Cache Bridge

South Leigh
Creek

Rainey

N

*Teton
River*

Driggs

Buxton Bridge

Boat Ramps

	River mile
Teton Creek	8
Buxton Bridge	13
Rainey	16
Cache Bridge	23
Harrop's Bridge	31
Spring Hollow	45
Teton Dam	62

Hazards

Felt Dam	37
Linderman Dam	50

Teton Creek

Targhee
National
Forest

Fox
Creek
West

Fox
Creek
East

33

Targhee
National
Forest

Victor

31

Pine Creek

Trail Creek

South Fork of the Snake

BEST FEATURES: Queen of the dry fly, the South Fork promises fly fishers an action-packed day, fantastic scenery and abundant wildlife.

SEASONS: Saturday, Memorial Day weekend to Nov. 30, Palisades Dam downstream to Heise measuring cable, mile above Byington boat ramp. Open year-round, Heise cable to confluence with Henry's Fork.

REGULATIONS: Two-trout limit; must release all species of trout between 8 and 16 inches. Barbless hooks recommended.

TROUT: Yellowstone and Snake River finespotted cutthroat in 12- to -18-inch class, a few 20 to 22 inches. Brown trout in 15- to 25-inch class. Idaho record brown trout — 26 lbs. 6 oz., 36.5 inches — in 1981. A few rainbow trout and rainbow-cutthroat hybrids in 12- to 24-inch class.

MILES: Palisades Dam to Henry's Fork: 64 miles. Palisades Dam to Conant Valley boat ramp: 15 miles. Conant Valley to Byington boat ramp: 25 miles. Byington boat ramp to Menan bridge: 25 miles.

CHARACTER: Big, pushy river with strong currents and hydraulics even at low flows. No white water; many side channels. Canoes not recommended on high spring flows. Waders should stick to side channels, riffles or edges of main channel. Float boaters should watch out for side channels blocked by debris and diversions for irrigation canals. Two most dangerous canal hazards are 1.5 miles below Byington boat ramp and 3 miles below Twin Bridges. At Conant Valley, the river enters scenic canyon with high, volcanic cliffs. Canyon ends below Heise bridge.

FLOWS: Spring runoff can exceed 20,000 cubic feet per second and affect river into July, but most years it peaks under 16,000 cfs by late-June. Summer flows often high due to irrigation releases up to 14,000 cfs. Fall flows reduced after Oct. 1 to about 5,000 cfs; drops to about 2,500 cfs in November. Winter, early spring flows are around 1,200 cfs.

ACCESS: Most easily fished in summer from boat; 11 public boat ramps. In Swan Valley a gravel road follows south bank. Above Twin Bridges a gravel road hugs north bank into lower canyon. Best wading, excellent dry fly action, is in fall; also late-winter, early-spring below Heise.

HATCHES: Stonefly hatch starts below Twin Bridges in late-June, works up through canyon by mid-July. Extending through July are profuse golden stone and willow fly hatches. Grasshoppers kick in end of July. Thick caddis fly, pale morning dun and Baetis hatches all season.

FLIES: Stonefly dries, stimulators and double-humpies, 4-6. Grasshoppers, 8-12. Yellow Sallies, elk hair caddis, stimulators, Wullfs and humpies, 10-16. Light Cahill, PMD, BWO, renegade and Adams, 12-16 in mid-season, 18-22 in fall. Dark stonefly nymphs, 4-8; Madame-X, super renegades, Zug bugs and woolly buggers , 6-14. Caddis emergers, pheasant tail and hare's ear nymphs, 12-16. Large woolly worms, muddlers, Matukas and streamers, plus egg patterns, in late-fall for browns.

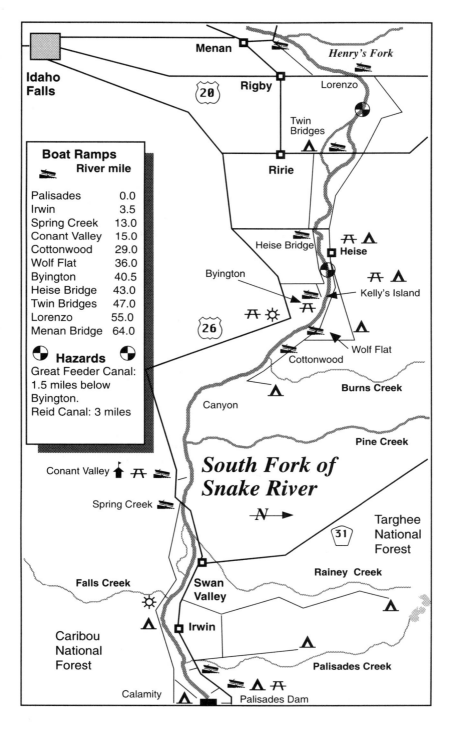

Idaho
Falls

Menan

Henry's Fork

20

Rigby

Lorenzo

Twin
Bridges

Ririe

Boat Ramps
River mile

Palisades	0.0
Irwin	3.5
Spring Creek	13.0
Conant Valley	15.0
Cottonwood	29.0
Wolf Flat	36.0
Byington	40.5
Heise Bridge	43.0
Twin Bridges	47.0
Lorenzo	55.0
Menan Bridge	64.0

◐ Hazards ◑
Great Feeder Canal:
1.5 miles below
Byington.
Reid Canal: 3 miles

Heise Bridge

Heise

Byington

Kelly's Island

26

Wolf Flat

Cottonwood

Burns Creek

Canyon

Pine Creek

South Fork of Snake River

→N→

Conant Valley

Targhee
National
Forest

31

Spring Creek

Rainey Creek

Falls Creek

Swan
Valley

Caribou
National
Forest

Irwin

Palisades Creek

Calamity

Palisades Dam

Dream Trip

Follow the salmon fly hatch from river to river

Few sights stir a fly caster's heart beat more than flights of salmon flies lumbering upstream to deposit their black, bomb-like sacs of precious eggs. They are a faithful harbinger of spring as heart warming as the swallows return to the mission of San Juan Capistrano.

These giant prehistoric-looking insects instill a fly fisher frenzy exceeded only by the slashing, explosive strikes of the trophy trout being pursued. Nymph fishers often forecast the approach of a hatch by turning over stream side rocks in search of the two-inch nymphs.

The big fly/big fish syndrome peaks during salmon fly hatches. In the Intermountain West, it's an early season phenomenon that brings even the most torpid angler out of hibernation. Fanatics welcome it as a trophy fishing orgy that can extend from mid-May through late-July in Greater Yellowstone's "golden circle" of trout streams. But, while nature provides, she doesn't always make it easy — or a sure bet. Local weather or spring runoff conditions can speed up or slow a hatch dramatically. For advance trip-planning, call an outfitter or fly tackle shop in March and April to see if it is going to be a cool or warm spring. A salmon fly hatch generally marks the waning of a stream's spring runoff and sets the stage for the season's other major hatches.

Actually, salmon fly is a misnomer. What causes the "Big Mac" attacks by trout are stoneflies, *Pteronarcys californica*. They were dubbed salmon flies because of the bright-orange coloration on portions of their bodies, particularly on the adult flying insect. Some westerners also call them "trout flies." A smaller species, the golden stonefly, *Acroneuria pacifica*, is golden-yellow on parts of its body. Sometimes referred to as "willow flies" or "yellow Sallies," golden stones hatch toward the end of a salmon fly hatch. They also come in a greater variety of sizes, and small, light-colored stimulator or elk hair caddis patterns can be effective options late into a season.

The key to fishing salmon flies is staying ahead of the game by finding the front of the hatch as it moves upstream. Otherwise, you'll be casting heavily weighted nymphs or "sofa pillow" dry flies to overstuffed cutthroat, rainbow and brown trout too laid back to care. Another effective strategy is to revisit these areas a week or so later when the fish are ready to take dries again. Or go back and work the golden stonefly hatch.

At a salmon fly hatch front, usually determined by the point where you can find only a few flying insects or nymph casings, your best bet is to cast nymphs toward the shoreline. Unlike mayflies and caddis flies, stoneflies do not emerge in mid-stream. They crawl across the stream bed to water's edge, climb near-by rocks or bushes and shuck their shell as they metamorphose into short-lived, airborne insects. Trout know the cycle and intercept the migrating nymphs.

Casting nymph patterns toward shore or parallel to it is relatively easy from a boat. Wading a shoreline in high water conditions can force right-handed casters to learn to use their left hands, or vice-versa. There's also the "chuck and duck" technique of casting heavily weighted nymphs into pocket waters behind boulders and other mid-stream structures.

Behind the vanguard of the emerging nymphs, dry flies come into play. Fishing a dry fly is the adrenaline-rush of a salmon fly hatch. A savage hit on a floating fly makes your heart skip a beat, followed by a shrilling reel releasing the fly line hooked by a monofilament thread to the fleeing fish. Late afternoon flights of salmon flies occur when egg-laying females ride the up welling swells of hot air flowing up from lower valleys through the canyons cut by the rivers. The egg sacs are deposited in rocky, fast-water stretches of the stream to begin the cycle anew. Many females also fall exhausted onto the water, or the bugs can be blown off stream side bushes by high winds.

Playing the dry fly action of a hatch is the icing on the cake. Nymph fishing with various imitations of this species is a year-round sport that peaks in spring. The nymphs live in the water for up to three years.

Finding the exactly right wet or dry pattern is less critical than confidence in its effectiveness and proper presentation. There are hundreds of patterns, ranging from super realistic to plain "buggy" looking impressions, and new ones are being created continuously. However, a variety of sizes, No. 8 to No. 2, is highly recommended. Golden stone, or yellow Sally, patterns range from No. 8 down to No. 14. Consult friends who tie their own flies or stop by a local fly tackle shop to find out what's hot.

Being where it's happening, staying at the leading edge of the hatch, is the ultimate key to success. Always call ahead to an outfitter nearest your destination before setting out, or consult with your local fly shop proprietor. Word of a hatch's progress gets out quick and is passed down the anglers network. Again, a good bet is to return a week or two after a hatch for another shot at dry fly action.

Shops to call in Idaho include All Seasons Angler or Hyde Pro Fly Shop in Idaho Falls, Henry's Fork Angler in Island Park, and South Fork Lodge or The Lodge at Palisades Creek in Swan Valley. In Montana, try Parks' Fly Shop in Gardiner, Montana's Master Anglers, Dan Bailey's or George Anderson's Yellowstone Anglers in Livingston, and Jacklin's Outfitters or Bud Lily's Trout Shop in West Yellowstone. In Wyoming, consult Jack Dennis Outdoor Shop, Wyoming Outfitter's High Country Flies or Westbank Anglers in Jackson.

Extending from mid-May to late-July, stonefly hatches occur on the Henry's Fork, Fall, Bighole, Madison, Yellowstone and Teton rivers, South Fork of the Snake and the Snake in Wyoming. Since many of the hatches overlap, it's possible to go to another river if conditions don't pan out on your first choice. Or you can be as gluttonous as the trout and try to do it all. Here's an itinerary for Greater Yellowstone waters. The dates indicate windows of opportunity, with emphasis on earliest starts:

Mid-May/Henry's Fork of Snake: Look for hatch on lower Henry's Fork as early as May 14 above Chester Dam. Often reaches Box Canyon in Island Park by Memorial Day weekend, the general season opener, and continues through Coffee Pot rapids into mid-June. Water can be high, but it's usually clear.

Early-June/Big Hole River: Look for start of good hatch of giant stoneflies and golden stoneflies end of first week of June between Divide, Mont., and Fish Trap Campground. Golden stonefly hatch continues above Fish Trap past first week of July. High water can be problem entire hatch.

Technically, this river is outside the Greater Yellowstone Ecosystem, but it is close enough for trips from Bozeman, Ennis and West Yellowstone for those who want to expand on their Madison or Gallatin adventures.

Mid-June/Gallatin River: Hatch on the lower Gallatin River can run from the second week of June to second week of July, with lots of help into mid-August from variety of golden stone and small stonefly hatches. Runoff usually peaks in early June and falls rapidly into July.

Mid-June/Teton River: For uncrowded fishing, seek out hatch in lower canyon above washed-out Teton Dam around June 14. It works up through canyon, continuing as late as July 21. Runoff is beginning to subside as this hatch progresses. Upper canyon access is very difficult. Super golden stonefly hatch keeps action going in lower canyon well into July.

Late-June/Fall River: Start looking around Ashton about June 21. Hatch continues to Cave Falls in Yellowstone National Park as late as July 14. High, muddy water can be problem at start of hatch, but it usually clears by early July.

Late-June/Madison River: You can usually chase the hatch from Ennis Lake to Quake Lake from mid-June to mid-July. Minor hatch on Madison in Yellowstone National Park, including lower Firehole canyon, occurs in late-June. Water is often high and discolored at start of hatch in lower stretches of Madison, but usually clears by first of July.

Late-June/Yellowstone River: You can start working your way up the river from Big Timber or Livingston the third week of June. Best bet is to follow hatch from Yankee Jim Canyon, below Gardiner, to Lower Falls in Yellowstone National Park during the first three weeks of July. High water can be problem at start of hatch, but it often clears by July 1. It may clear sooner above Lamar River in canyon, but the Lamar also can become high and roily following summer storms and discolor the Yellowstone in Black Canyon. Smaller hatch also occurs on Yellowstone above Upper Falls, and often coincides with the opening of that stretch to fishing on July 15.

Hatches in the park can extend into the Lamar River and the Gardner River during the first three weeks of July.

Fourth of July/South Fork of Snake (Idaho): The "fireworks" on the South Fork begin in late-June below Heise. Peak of hatch often occurs in lower canyon around the Fourth of July, with action continuing upstream as far as Swan Valley for another two or three weeks. Water levels vary with irrigation releases from Palisades Dam. Golden stone, yellow Sally and small stonefly hatches overlap giant stones and provide good action into August with elk hair caddis, willow fly, humpies and stimulators.

July/Snake River (Wyoming): Start looking for sporadic hatch in the Grand Canyon below Hoback River around first week of July. It works its way upstream through Grand Teton National Park by third week of month. Sporadic nature of hatch makes nymph patterns more effective than stonefly dries — although large, high-riding dry fly patterns are always a staple on the river from Jackson Lake to Grand Canyon of the Snake. Water levels vary with irrigation releases from Jackson Lake.

Late-June to early July salmon fly hatches on the Gros Ventre, Hoback, Grey's and Salt rivers in western Wyoming are worth pursuing, too. All four of these tributaries of the Snake are often overlooked except by local fly fishers in-the-know. Classic mountain streams, they are much easier to wade than the powerful Snake, which is the realm of guided float-boaters at this time.

Western Wyoming

Realm of robust cutthroat, majestic mountains

With the majestic Teton Mountains dominating the horizon, western Wyoming is a land of spectacular vistas. Its wild and robust trout are fully up to the task of matching their picture-postcard environs. Both amplify the rhapsody of this incredible playground of sagebrush flats, forested foothills, snow-capped peaks and sparkling clear waters. Wildlife viewing opportunities of Grand Teton National Park, Jackson Hole and the Teton Wilderness rival the numbers and variety more commonly associated with Yellowstone National Park.

This is where Greater Yellowstone's waters separate on their journeys to the sea. The parting of the waters occurs at a spring-fed trickle that splits and spills off Two Ocean Pass on the Continental Divide above Jackson. Atlantic Creek flows northeast to join the Yellowstone River, larger than the region's three rivers that create the Missouri, main tributary of the Mississippi. Pacific Creek flows southwest to join the Snake River, largest tributary of the Columbia.

The Snake River finespotted cutthroat is the predominate trout on the Pacific side of the mountains. Its first cousin, the Yellowstone cutthroat, also inhabit some of these waters but its realm of dominance is in the park on the Atlantic side of the divide.

A subspecies still being studied by biologists, the Snake River finespotted is unique in its ability to co-exist with its parent species. Its spotting pattern is heavier with many smaller spots than the Yellowstone cutthroat. Many consider it less gullible and a stronger fighter than its cousin. Finespotted cutthroat occur naturally throughout the drainage, and Wyoming Game and Fish's fish stocking program supplements populations in some tributaries of the Snake. Also present in the basin, in varying population numbers, are brown, rainbow and brook trout in the streams, and lake trout or mackinaw in Jackson Lake and a few other lakes. Whitefish are plentiful throughout the basin.

The Snake is a big, brawling river and demands respect. It fishes best from a boat, and newcomers or inexperienced boaters are advised to make their first floats with guides or friends who know the river. Fly casters who prefer to wade should stick to quiet, shallow sections of the river and side channels. Good access is found near boat ramps and bridges. Spring runoff is often late, so plan to fish the Snake in late-summer or fall.

More accommodating to wading, and virtually undiscovered, are a number of fine mountain streams flowing into the Snake. Good prospects closest to Jackson are the upper Gros Ventre River and Flat Creek. A demanding spring creek fishery, the latter doesn't open until August 1.

South of Jackson, the Salt and Grey's rivers flow into Palisades Reservoir at Alpine. The Salt is most productive fishing from a small boat or canoe. The Grey's is a perfect camping getaway for family fishing parties or neophyte fly fishers who want to hone their skills in relative solitude. In between Jackson and Alpine, the Hoback River enters the Snake. It is most popular during the salmon fly hatch, and in late-summer and fall. Granite Creek, a tributary of the Hoback, is a classic, small mountain stream.

North of Jackson is the Teton Wilderness, preserved for ventures afoot or on horse back. Its most tempting cutthroat fishing — a long way up the trail and over the divide — is the upper meadow section of the Yellowstone River and Thorofare Creek. On the west slopes of the divide, good streams to consider are Pacific Creek and the Buffalo Fork River.

Jackson has a host of well-stocked fly tackle shops and outfitters available to fill your equipment needs or help guide your explorations.

The other major drainage in western Wyoming's Yellowstone country is the Big Horn basin. Premier fly fishing streams on the east side of the park are the North Fork of the Shoshone and Clark's Fork of the Yellowstone rivers. Both offer comfortable wading in their upper reaches and harbor moderate-sized fish, with good chances for souvenir photographs of honorable fish. Dry fly fishing in the fall can be especially memorable. Primary action is on cutthroat, rainbow and brook trout. The lower Clark's Fork holds a few browns; their numbers are stronger in the lower North Fork.

Paralleled by the main highway to the park's East Entrance, the North Fork tends to be crowded at the height of the tourist season. Fishing is superlative and the atmosphere more serene after Labor Day. The Clark's Fork is more remote and allows chances for solitude even during the busy season. In autumn, it is a scenic wonder land with fine dry fly fishing.

Dominated by the Absaroka and Beartooth mountains, this basin's wilderness scenery matches the Swiss Alps. The middle of the Clark's Fork plunges through one of the deepest, most picturesque gorges in North America. High above timberline are hundreds of emerald green alpine lakes that hold mostly brook trout, as well as cutthroat, rainbow and golden trout, and a few grayling. Access to the lakes on the Wyoming side of the Beartooth Wilderness is relatively easy from trails along the Scenic Beartooth Highway on U.S. 12. Those planning to venture into the Absaroka Wilderness might want to consider a guided trip by horse back with an outfitter.

The frontier resort town of Cody is the main service hub for this area and the eastern gateway community for Yellowstone. Be sure to visit its superb Old West museums. The Clark's Fork also can be reached from the park's Northwest Entrance, and Cooke City and Red Lodge, Montana.

Public access is no problem in the parks or national forests, and at designated state access sites. Boaters can float streams passing through private lands, but waders must obtain permission to fish. The water belongs to the state, but ranchers and farmers own the stream beds on their land.

Snake River

BEST FEATURES: Robust river, filled with unique Snake River finespotted cutthroat, flows past spellbinding Grand Tetons; abundant wildlife. Feisty cutthroat good to beginners; present ample challenges to experts.
SEASON: Open to fishing April 1 through October 31.
REGULATIONS: 1,000 feet below Jackson Lake Dam to Wilson bridge, no bait, 3-fish limit, none between 12 and 18 inches, only 1 over 18 inches; Wilson bridge to West Table Boat Ramp, 3-fish limit, only 1 over 12 inches.
TROUT: Great fishing for finespotted cutthroat in 12- to 16-inch class; a few may exceed 22 inches in Grand Teton National Park stretch and in canyon below Hoback River. Some brook trout in tributary areas. Large cutthroat spawners run upstream from Jackson Lake in spring; a few browns in fall.
MILES: 130 in Wyoming. Source south of Yellowstone Park to Jackson Lake, 40 miles. Dam to Moose, 25 miles. Moose to Wilson Bridge: 15 miles. Wilson to South Park Bridge: 13 miles. South Park to Astoria: 12 miles. Astoria to West Table Creek: 10 miles. Table Creek to Alpine: 15 miles.
CHARACTER: Broad, rapid free-stone river with many channels in park. Major whitewater in Grand Canyon above Palisades Reservoir. Below Jackson Dam, river flows though serene Oxbow section to Pelican Creek, where pace picks up down through wide, braided floodplain cut into deep glacial deposits; channels change annually, log jams common. Single channel from South Park to Astoria, then river braids again. Below West Table, deep rocky chutes and rapids in canyon include Class IV Lunch Counter.
FLOWS: Jackson Lake Dam controls flows; spring runoff often starts late; November to April, about 1,000 cubic feet per second; late May through July, 5,000 to 15,000 cfs; August through September, 2,000 to 5,000 cfs.
ACCESS: Fishing blown-out most years mid-May to early-July. Best fishing is from boat with outfitter guide; inexperienced boaters should float river only with someone who knows it well. Wading easy above lake but often difficult, dangerous below dam; stick to side channels and banks near boat ramps, bridges and along flood-control dikes. Grand Canyon is impossible. Unlimited access in Grand Teton Park; private lands limit access in Jackson Hole; Bridger-Teton National Forest boundary about 2 miles below Hoback.
HATCHES: Matching a hatch not a major factor on this river; look for Baetis and midges in April and in late-fall; sporadic stone fly hatch in mid-July; golden stones, caddis, PMD, green and gray drakes later in summer. Large terrestrial, caddis and attractor patterns most effective August into October.
FLIES: Elk hair caddis, Wulffs, Trudes, stimulators, humpies, double-humpies, yellow Sallies, hoppers, 10-8; western red quill, green or gray drakes, 12-10; BWO, PMD, parachute Adams, 14-16. Black and golden stone nymphs, rubber-legs, woolly buggers,10-4; beadheads, prince, hare's ear nymphs, 12-14. Muddlers, Zonkers, Matuka streamers, 8-2.

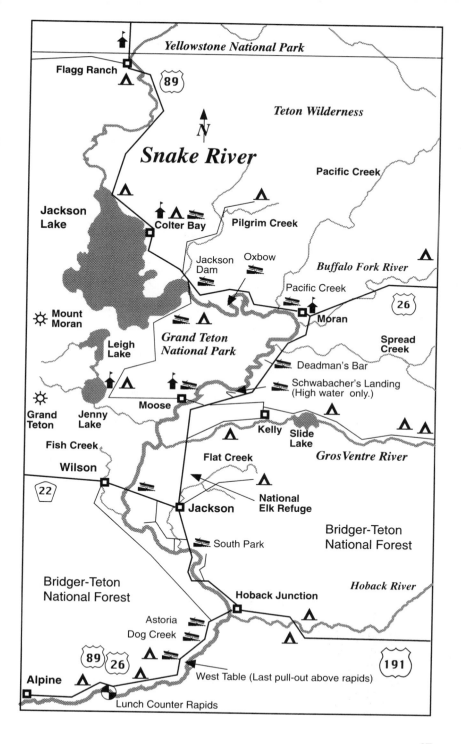

Yellowstone National Park

Flagg Ranch

89

Snake River

N

Teton Wilderness

Pacific Creek

Jackson Lake

Colter Bay

Pilgrim Creek

Jackson Dam

Oxbow

Buffalo Fork River

Pacific Creek

Moran

26

Mount Moran

Grand Teton National Park

Spread Creek

Leigh Lake

Deadman's Bar

Schwabacher's Landing
(High water only.)

Grand Teton

Jenny Lake

Moose

Kelly

Slide Lake

Gros Ventre River

Fish Creek

Wilson

Flat Creek

22

Jackson

National Elk Refuge

Bridger-Teton National Forest

South Park

Bridger-Teton National Forest

Hoback River

Hoback Junction

Astoria

Dog Creek

89 26

West Table (Last pull-out above rapids)

191

Alpine

Lunch Counter Rapids

Salt, Grey's and Hoback rivers

BEST FEATURES: Fun-filled mountain streams perfect for family outings or solitary getaways. Tributaries of the Snake, all three permit easy wading in pursuit of scrappy wild trout. Close enough to Jackson and Idaho Falls for pleasant day trips; many public campgrounds for longer stays.

SEASONS: Salt above Highway. 238 bridge closed Nov. 1 through Dec. 31.

REGULATIONS: See WG&F regulations for slot limits and bag limits on key stretches of Salt and Grey's rivers.

TROUT: Grey's and Hoback are realm of Snake River finespotted cutthroat in 8- to 14-inch range; some larger fish in deeper pools; a few brook trout in upper Hoback. Salt holds a few rainbows and brookies, but mostly cutthroat and browns in 10- to 16-inch range; chance for trophy browns year-round, especially during late-fall spawning run out of Palisades Reservoir.

MILES: All three flow between 50 and 60 miles from headwaters to confluence with Snake or Palisades Reservoir at Alpine.

CHARACTER: The Salt drops from about 6,600 feet in Salt River Range south of Smoot to 5,400 feet at reservoir; lower 30 miles meander through farm and ranch country of Star Valley. Comfortable to wade in places. Best fishing from small boat or canoe, especially below The Narrows where channels often lined with willows, or too deep or strong to wade. Grey's rises at 7,000 feet east of Smoot, flows down narrow valley between Salt River and Wyoming mountain ranges; picks up flows of Little Grey's River east of Alpine. Its crystalline waters drop in strings of riffles and runs, with intermittent logjams, pocket waters and cutbank pools. Hoback drops from about 8,000 feet in Wyoming Range southeast of Hoback Junction to about 6,100 feet at Snake. Upper river emerges from mountains, flows briefly through a sagebrush plain and turns sharply northwest on its course through narrow valley into canyon. Mostly riffles and runs, intermittent pocket waters, cutbank pools; some deep pools, rock gardens in canyon.

FLOWS: Spring runoff sooner, clears earlier on Salt, usually by late-May or early June. Hoback's runoff is highest, most turbulent, often lasts from May into July. Grey's runoff begins to subside in mid-June, clears by July.

ACCESS: 17 public access sites to Salt along U.S. 89. Grey's paralleled by forest roads; top half can be very slick when wet. U.S. 191 hugs Hoback in canyon, forest roads parallel upper river; bottom of canyon private land.

HATCHES: Caddis, golden stoneflies, willow flies, June and July on Salt; hoppers, late-summer. Giant stoneflies on Hoback, early July. Traditional high-floating dry flies, small nymphs work through season on all three rivers.

FLIES: Stoneflies, 2-6; golden stones, 6-8; hoppers, 6-10; elk hair caddis, yellow Sallies, stimulators, humpies, 10-14; Wulffs, renegade, Adams, PMD, BWO,12-16. Soft- hackle, hare's ear, prince, pheasant tail nymphs, 10-14; stone fly nymphs, woolly buggers, muddlers, streamers, 2-10.

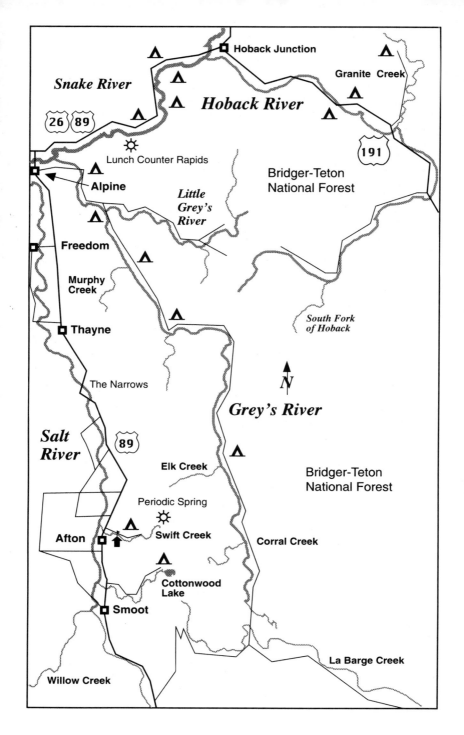

Snake River

Hoback Junction

Granite Creek

26 89

Lunch Counter Rapids

Alpine

Hoback River

Bridger-Teton
National Forest

191

Little
Grey's
River

Freedom

Murphy
Creek

Thayne

South Fork
of Hoback

The Narrows

N

Grey's River

Salt
River

89

Bridger-Teton
National Forest

Elk Creek

Periodic Spring

Afton

Swift Creek

Corral Creek

Cottonwood
Lake

Smoot

La Barge Creek

Willow Creek

North Fork of Shoshone River

BEST FEATURES: Scenic mountain stream on East Road to Yellowstone National Park. Popular with families, it is filled with wild trout, easily waded. Good-fishing tributaries of North Fork include Grinnell, Clearwater, Sweetwater, Elk Fork and Eagle creeks. South Fork basically a carbon copy of North Fork but access very limited due to passage through private lands.

SEASON: Open year-round; except Gibbs Bridge upstream to Newton Creek, closed to fishing April 1 through June 30.

REGULATIONS: 3 trout per day or in possession, only 1 over 20 inches.

TROUT: Yellowstone cutthroat and rainbows in 10- to 15-inch class, a few larger; some brown trout on lower end and brook trout in upper reaches.

MILES: Area of prime interest and best access is the 35 miles between Pahaska Teepee at East Entrance of the park and Buffalo Bill Reservoir.

CHARACTER: North Fork emerges from remote Absaroka Wilderness east of park and flows in shallow rocky glides, riffles and runs, intermittent cutbank pools, through heavily wooded valley to Buffalo Bill Reservoir. Easy wading along U.S. 20/14; cobble floor can be slippery. Headwaters reach and tributaries in remote wilderness areas best fished with a guide or friends who know the country. Deep canyon below reservoir is narrow, rocky, difficult to access. River continues in northeasterly direction through rolling, high desert basin past Cody to Big Horn River. Due to geothermal features, Shoshone was called ``Stinking River" by John Colter, first white man in Yellowstone-Teton region. Wapiti wilderness country was favorite playground of William ``Buffalo Bill" Cody and President Teddy Roosevelt.

FLOWS: Runoff can extend into July; best fishing in late-summer and autumn. Flows below reservoir controlled by dam for irrigation interests.

ACCESS: U.S. 20/14 skirts river from park entrance to Cody. All but a few miles of river above reservoir in Shoshone National Forest. Numerous trailheads provide access to upper river, tributaries and alpine lakes, north in Absaroka Wilderness and south in Washakie Wilderness; no vehicles allowed. County and forest roads skirt southwest shore of reservoir and South Fork, which passes through a few sections of public lands.

HATCHES: Stone fly (salmonfly) and golden stones, June and July. Baetis (BWO) early spring, mid-summer, late-fall. Pale morning dun (PMD), June into October. Caddis flies, June through September. Grasshopper and beetle action is best in August, September. Excellent dry fly action on small mayflies and attractor patterns in September and October; summer tourists are long gone and elk hunters are distracted by other pursuits.

FLIES: Stone fly, 6-10; golden stones, 8-12. Grasshoppers, 6-10; elk hair caddis, yellow Sallies, stimulators, humpies, 10-14; Wulffs, renegade, Adams, PMD, BWO, 12-16. Soft- hackle, hare's ear, prince, pheasant tail nymphs, 10-14; woolly buggers, rubber-legs, muddlers, streamers, 4-10.

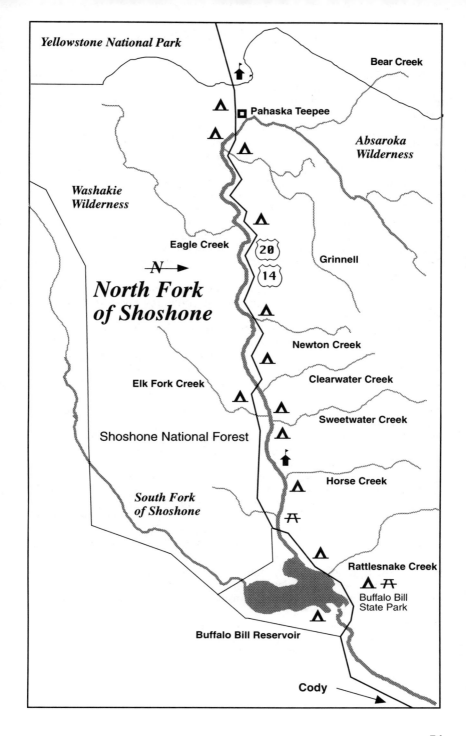

Yellowstone National Park

Bear Creek

Pahaska Teepee

Absaroka
Wilderness

Washakie
Wilderness

Eagle Creek

20

14

Grinnell

N

North Fork
of Shoshone

Newton Creek

Clearwater Creek

Elk Fork Creek

Sweetwater Creek

Shoshone National Forest

Horse Creek

South Fork
of Shoshone

Rattlesnake Creek

Buffalo Bill
State Park

Buffalo Bill Reservoir

Cody

Clark's Fork of the Yellowstone

BEST FEATURES: Wild and Scenic River east of Yellowstone National Park. Opportunity to pursue accommodating wild trout in virtual solitude no longer possible in the madding crowds associated with park's streams.

SEASON: Open all year; inaccessible from Cooke City until end of May.

REGULATIONS: Bag limit from state line to Reef Creek is 6 trout per day, none over 8 inches; artificial flies and lures only. From Reef Creek through canyon to Shoshone National Forest boundary, bag limit is 3 trout per day, only one over 12 inches. From forest boundary to state line, bag limit is 6 trout per day, no size restrictions.

TROUT: Rainbows 12- to 14-inch in upper reaches, a few 16-incher; plus a few cutthroat and brook trout. In canyon, rainbows in 12- to 14-inch class with chance for 18-incher. Lower stretch, a few brown trout; stocked with 8- to 12-inch cutthroats and rainbows, as well as graylings. Crandall Creek holds cutthroat up to 20 inches; Sunlight Creek, a few 14-inch brook trout.

MILES: Headwaters in Beartooth Mountains above Cooke City, Mont. Flows northeast 66 miles in Wyoming and continues another 72 miles in Montana to join Yellowstone River.

CHARACTER: From Montana - Wyoming state line to Crandall Creek, 16 miles, river meanders through high-mountain, forested valley. Flows are gentle and easily waded expect for occasional deep runs and pools. At Crandall Creek, it plunges into deep, scenic canyon, runs 20 miles through boulder-strewn pocket waters, deep pools and strong eddies; waterfalls in middle of 1,200-foot canyon make it inaccessible. At canyon mouth, it flows into sagebrush desert and meanders to state line; best fishing here in July.

FLOWS: Spring runoff can extend through June into early July. Steady summer flows may pick up again from autumn storms.

ACCESS: Public access in Shoshone National Forest. River parallels U.S. 212 and Wyo. 296 in upper reaches. Upper section comfortable wading. Canyon section requires rock scrambling; don't wear waders. Trailheads into canyon at Crandall, Russell, Reef and Dead Indian creeks. Road leaves river at Sunlight Creek. Reach lower end of canyon via gravel road (Wyo. 292) by turning west off Wyo. 120 just south of village of Clark. Lower river runs mostly through private land, look for public access signs.

HATCHES: Sporadic stonefly hatch makes nymphs more effective than dries. Caddis flies more common than mayflies. Grasshopper action in upper reach best in August and September. Excellent dry fly action on small mayflies, chance for solitude, in September and October.

FLIES: Tan and olive elk hair caddis, yellow and orange stimulators, PMD, BWO, Adams, Wulffs, renegades and small green drake, 12 -16; hoppers, 8-12. Stonefly and golden stone nymphs, woolly buggers, 4-8. Fish caddis larva, emergers, and prince and hare's ear nymphs, 12-16, as dropper flies.

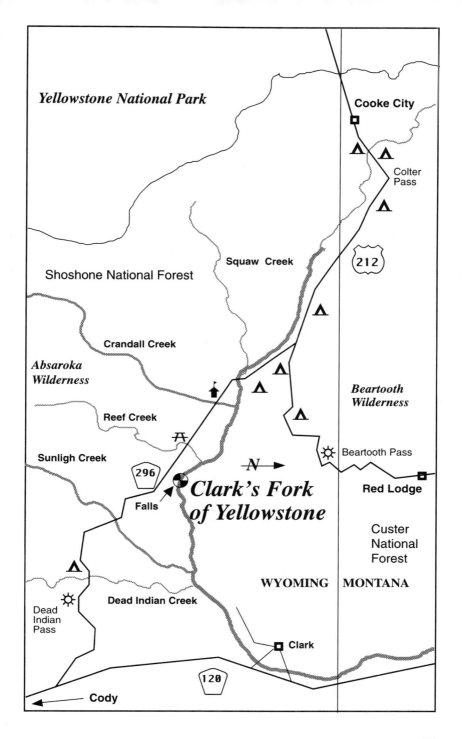

Yellowstone National Park

Cooke City

Colter Pass

Shoshone National Forest

Squaw Creek

212

Crandall Creek

Absaroka
Wilderness

Beartooth
Wilderness

Reef Creek

Sunligh Creek

296

Beartooth Pass

Red Lodge

N

Clark's Fork
of Yellowstone

Falls

Custer
National
Forest

WYOMING   MONTANA

Dead Indian Creek

Dead
Indian
Pass

Clark

120

Cody

Other adventures:

Upper Yellowstone, Gros Ventre, Flat Creek

Jackson Lake's Colter Bay is named for John Colter, a member of the Lewis and Clark Expedition who stayed on in the West when the Corps returned from the Pacific. Campfire stories of his solo journey through the Teton-Yellowstone country during the winter of 1807-1808 were greeted as the first of many tall tales Mountain Men brought back to the East. For others following in his foot steps, the steaming, fountaining geysers and bubbling mud pots of Yellowstone inspired the name, "Colter's Hell."

The fur trappers stripped the mountain streams of beaver by the late-1840s. Later explorers, like John Fremont and Benjamin Bonneville, charted pathways to the West Coast. Pioneer settlers followed, and many dropped off to stay in places like Jackson Hole and Star Valley. Fortunately, our forefathers had the vigilance to preserve Yellowstone in 1872. The movement to preserve the Tetons and their environs blossomed in the late-1930s and continued into the mid-1980s.

Thus, even today, it is possible to feel the sense of awe Colter savored when he topped Togwotee Pass and saw the fang-like crest of the Tetons gnawing the western horizon. Most modern explorers already know of the alpine splendors preserved in Grand Teton National Park. Less known, but better suited to the Mountain Man mode of travel, is the Teton Wilderness Area north of Jackson. Wise hikers and horseback riders venturing into this wild, remote forest filled with streams and lakes carry a fly rod.

Following are some backcountry jaunts with fishing in mind.

Teton Wilderness / Upper Yellowstone:

For incredibly memorable fishing, hike or ride a horse to the upper Yellowstone River and Thorofare Creek. A bonus at the end of the trail, 25 to 30 miles long, is Bridger Lake. Fishing is excellent in all three for Yellowstone cutthroat in the 14- to 18-inch range, with chances for a true lunker. The window of opportunity is short. Most of the fish are spring spawners that run up from Yellowstone Lake. The spawners begin dropping out of the system by August, but heavy-bodied resident cutthroat reside here, too. Spring runoff peaks in late-June. Mosquitoes can be pesky past July. But by staying south of the park border in the Hawk's Rest area, you can fish earlier than the park's July 15 opener. (See map on Page 26.) Although it is a classic meadow stream, this is not rocket science fishing. Standard caddis, mayfly, attractor and terrestrial patterns will produce in most situations. Bag and possession limit is 2 cutthroat, only 1 over 20 inches.

Wildlife is abundant, including grizzly bears. Don't hike alone.

Trails to Yellowstone Thorofare are up Pacific Creek, and up North Fork of Buffalo Fork River, starting from Turpin Meadow. Both trails meet at 8,200-foot Two Ocean Pass. A third route west of Cody is on the South Fork of the Shoshone. Outfitters are based in Jackson and Cody. Obtain Forest Service's Teton Wilderness map at Jackson or Cody office.

Less arduous fishing trails in the Teton Wilderness include:

Pacific Creek — One of main access routes into wilderness; rated as good fishing for 10- to 16-inch cutthroat, also contains brook trout.

Gravel Lake — An 8-mile hike, reached by taking north fork on Pacific Creek trail; rated as good fishing for 10- to 13-inch cutthroat.

Buffalo Fork River and North Fork — Best above Turpin Meadow Campground and on North Fork; rated as good fishing for 8- to 16-inch cutthroat and rainbows, also contains brook trout.

Enos Lake — Largest lake in wilderness; 12-mile hike from Box Creek trailhead in Buffalo Valley; rated as good fishing for 12- to 14-inch cutthroat.

Toppings Lakes — An hour's hike from trailhead at end of forest road across from Cunningham Cabin in Park; first lake rated as excellent for 8- to 16-inch grayling; second lake tougher fishing for 12- to 16-inch grayling.

Grand Teton National Park:

Jackson Lake is 90 percent lake trout, also holds cutthroat and a few browns. Jenny and Leigh lakes offers good fishing for lake trout and cutthroat. Wade or canoe shallows along shores and at inlets; best after ice-out in spring and again in fall. Long hikes into alpine lakes mean they are mostly un-fished. Wyoming license required; obtain park regulations.

Gros Ventre River:

The upper Gros Ventre River, above Kelly, is a late-summer, early fall fishery that tests fly fishers more than other streams in the basin. Its crystal clear flows demand more finesse in presentation, longer, delicate leaders and small flies. But it has a late stone fly hatch around the second week of July, and you can often score by splatting a grasshopper into a strategic holding area later in the season. It is easily waded in most places, and lone wolf-types who hike a short distance from the road find secluded bends to fish. Pocket waters below Slide Lake offer the best rainbow fishing, but cutthroat remain the dominate fish in this exceptional mountain stream. It is rated as good fishing for 10- to 16-inch fish, with a few going 22 inches.

Flat Creek:

Devotees of demanding spring creek-like fishing line up for the Aug. 1 opening of Flat Creek. Its fishing is more serene long before it closes Oct. 31. Flat Creek bisects the National Elk Refuge, just north of Jackson, flowing through a meadow marsh. The creek's spongy banks telegraph your footsteps. So, often times, your approach has to be as delicate as your presentation. Small fly technicians do well casting to feeding fish with long rods. But grasshoppers and crane flies also score along cutbanks, and occasionally large nymphs. It is rated as good fishing for 8- to 20-inch cutthroat. Fly fishing only, with a 1-fish limit, which must exceed 20 inches. Creek in Jackson above U.S.191 bridge is for kids only, under age of 14.

Southwestern Montana

Wild trout match Old West spirit of Big Sky state

A leader in wild trout management, Montana embraced its philosophy of natural stream fisheries more than 20 years ago. It preserved a treasure trove of trout streams in the process, with Greater Yellowstone's rivers among its best, and the state gained a world renowned reputation among fly fishers.

This success and accompanying media hype heralding the attractions of "The Last Best Place" bring new challenges. Future fisheries managers are presented as great a challenge in people management as they are in continued restoration and protection of wild trout habitat.

Summer is most popular but it is not the only time to fish in Montana, or elsewhere in the Intermountain West. Before spring runoff kicks in, early season fishing — late-March through April — surprises many newcomers to this burgeoning time of year. After summer crowds depart, the suspended days of autumn forever captivate those who linger on the glittering waters of this golden season.

In the secluded niches of the region's river bottoms and canyons, the weather can be as cooperative year-round as the trout. Pleasant warming days of spring renew the spirit. Crisp cool days of fall delight the soul. Winter's occasional temperate episodes entice devout trout hunters seeking an antidote to cabin fever.

The narrow window of opportunity in Greater Yellowstone's mountain-river country is on its alpine lakes. Above timber line, ice break up occurs most years in late-June, early July, but snow fall threatens again by September or early October.

No exploration of this northern extension of the ecosystem would be complete without experiencing the Beartooth Mountains. Called the "roof of Montana," the Beartooths harbor more than 400 trout-filled lakes dotting a broad exposed plateau with peaks exceeding 11,000 feet. To the west and south are the ice sculptured crags of the Absaroka Mountains and their more solitary wilderness retreats.

A sprawling land of contrasts, Montana offers yet another challenge. One of the ultimate tests of fly fishing skills in North America awaits expert casters south of Livingston at Paradise Valley's internationally acclaimed spring creeks. A rod fee is charged on Armstrong and Nelson's creeks; the reward is stalking and netting large wary trout. Reservations are required at the height of the tourist season, but opportunities to get on the creeks are easier in early spring and late-fall.

For free-roaming fly fishers, these prime spawning tributaries contribute thousands of new recruits annually to the phenomenal fishery of the Yellowstone River. Its ranking as a world-class fly fishing stream was secured by hard fought battles to preserve it as the longest free-flowing river in the Lower 48. From Gardiner, at the park's border, down through Paradise Valley to Big Timber, the Yellowstone is one of the great rivers of the West. Good trout fishing continues downstream to Billings.

Its upper waters still hold strong populations of Yellowstone cutthroat. Below the turbulent waters of Yankee Jim Canyon, rainbows and browns are more common and present more challenges.

The Boulder River joins the Yellowstone at Big Timber. It is typical of the rock laden streams flowing off the alpine heights of the Absaroka-Beartooth Wilderness. Its two main tributaries, East Boulder and West Boulder, also offer excellent fishing. Just over the ridge to the east is the Stillwater River, a carbon-copy of the Boulder, that joins the Yellowstone at Columbus.

Flowing out of the northeast corner of the park is the Gallatin River, one of the three tributaries that form the Missouri River west of Bozeman. A classic mountain trout stream, the Gallatin is smaller and easier to wade than most larger Western rivers. Below the Big Sky ski resort it plunges through a picturesque canyon popular with whitewater rafters during spring runoff. Fly fishers in the know find its subdued waters of early spring or late-fall a joy to fish in relative seclusion.

East Gallatin River, northwest of Bozeman, is gaining a reputation as a challenging brown trout stream. Much of its willow-lined course flows through farm land. Check locally for public access sites and boat ramps.

Perhaps most famous of all in the lexicon of Montana's revered trout streams is the Madison. Exiting the park at West Yellowstone it joins the Gallatin and Jefferson at Three Forks to form the Missouri.

Thanks to droves of so-called yuppie fly fishers flocking to its celebrated salmon fly hatch, the tiny resort town of Ennis is known as Tuxedo Junction in late-June, early July. But summer hordes miss the Madison's often spectacular late-fall and early spring fishing. It fishes well on balmy days of winter, too. In late summer, float-tubing trophy hunters focus on Hebgen Lake during the Trico hatch. Their quarry is "gulpers," cruising pods of monster trout gulping down swarms of the tiny black mayflies.

Confirmation in 1994 of the presence of whirling disease cast a shroud of gloom over the Madison. Losses of 70 to 90 percent in its rainbow population were attributed to the disease. Still, reports of the river's demise were premature. Decent populations of rainbows remain and recruitment of young fish improved in 1995, a wet year. Browns, largely unaffected by the disease, appear to be filling new niches and growing larger.

Studies of the disease's threat are ongoing. Other contributing factors to trout losses worth considering are a decade of drought and mismanagement of river flows from Hebgen Dam. The jury is still out ... stay tuned.

Gallatin River

BEST FEATURES: Classic mountain trout stream, smaller and easier to wade than larger Western rivers. Picturesque canyon, abundant wildlife.

SEASON: Open to fishing year-round in Montana; winter closure in park.

REGULATIONS: No boat fishing, Yellowstone Park to East Gallatin River. Montana limit is 5 trout, only 1 over 18 inches; release grayling. In park, catch- and-release cutthroat; 2-fish limit on both rainbow, browns. No boats.

TROUT: Park waters contain small Yellowstone cutthroat, rainbows and hybrids; a few browns to 18 inches. Below Taylor Creek to Gallatin Gateway, mostly rainbows and browns that run 10 to 16 inches; hatchery grayling. Large browns enter lower river from Missouri during fall spawning run.

MILES: 115 miles from headwaters in park to Missouri. Mile 0: Gallatin Lake headwaters; Mile 26: Park boundary; Mile 46: Big Sky; Mile 70: Gallatin Canyon Mouth; Mile 72: Williams Bridge; Mile 82: Highway 84 bridge; Mile 104: Nixon Bridge and East Gallatin River; Mile 115: confluence with Missouri.

CHARACTER: Tumbling headwaters in park widen with tributary flows. Ten-mile stretch nearest U.S. 191 runs through broad, bowl-like valley in series of swift runs, shallow riffles, and occasional long, slow pools and cutbanks. Wider and swifter below Taylor Creek with fast runs, occasional riffles and strings of long pools. Narrow scenic canyon below Big Sky filled with boulder-choked rapids and fast-flowing chutes, intermittent deep runs and pools, a few riffles. At canyon mouth river spills into broad plain, slows and meanders through farmland. Numerous irrigation diversion dams may dry up some channels in summer. Picks up East Gallatin River at Manhattan.

FLOWS: Spring runoff begins in April, peaks around 4,000 the end of May and falls rapidly through June to about 1,200 cfs by July and 800 cfs by August. Late-fall and winter flows around 600 cfs to less than 500 cfs.

ACCESS: U.S. 191 parallels most of river. Full public access in park and Gallatin National Forest. Mostly private land below canyon mouth, with four main bridge access sites. Stay in stream bed or below highwater line to avoid trespassing. Trails in park to Fan, Bacon Rind and Specimen creeks.

HATCHES: Giant stonefly, late-June to mid-July; golden stones, July; and yellow Sally, July into mid-August. Western March Brown, late-March – April. Baetis (BWO), March-April, mid-July and August, and late-fall. Pale morning dun (PMD), July. Caddis (tan, brown, olive, black) April through September. Tricos, August. Hoppers, July - September. Midges, all year.

FLIES: Salmonfly, 2-6; golden stone, 4-10; yellow Sally, 12-14. BWO, 18-26. PMD, 14-18. March Brown, 12-14. Caddis, 14-20. Tricos, 20-24. Midges, 18-24. Elk hair caddis, stimulators, humpies,14-20. Hoppers, 6-12. Ants, beetles, 14-20. Wullfs, Trudes, renegades, 12-16. Stonefly, golden stone nymphs, rubber-legs, woolly buggers, 8-12. Hare's ear nymph, Zug bug, prince, green or yellow soft-hackle partridge, caddis emergers, 10-14.

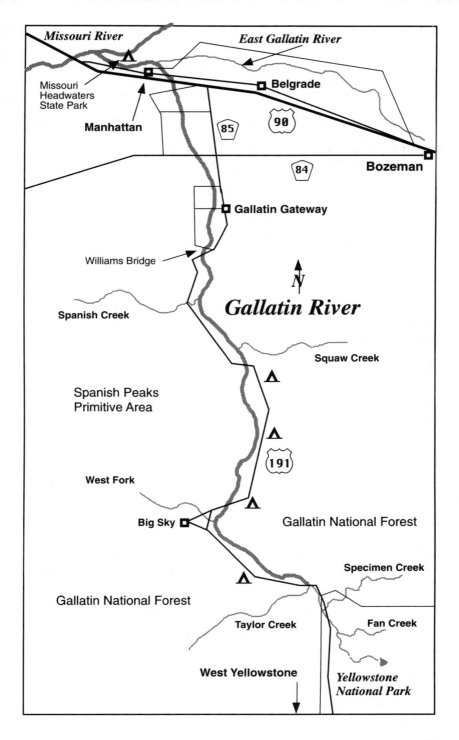

Missouri River

East Gallatin River

Missouri Headwaters State Park

Belgrade

Manhattan

85

90

84

Bozeman

Gallatin Gateway

Williams Bridge

N

Gallatin River

Spanish Creek

Squaw Creek

Spanish Peaks Primitive Area

191

West Fork

Big Sky

Gallatin National Forest

Specimen Creek

Gallatin National Forest

Taylor Creek

Fan Creek

West Yellowstone

Yellowstone National Park

Madison River

BEST FEATURES: Most famous salmon fly hatch in West comes off in late-June, early July but summer hordes miss often spectacular late-fall and early spring fishing. Hebgen Lake float-tubers pursue Trico "gulpers."
SEASON: Above Hebgen Lake, third Saturday of May through Nov. 30; Hebgen Lake to Varney Bridge, year-round; Varney Bridge to Ennis Lake, third Saturday of May through Nov. 30; Ennis Dam to mouth, year-round.
REGULATIONS: Quake Lake to Varney Bridge, catch-and-release all trout; Varney Bridge to Ennis Lake, catch-and-release rainbows, 5-fish limit on browns, only 1 over 18 inches; standard limit on rest of river, lakes. No boat fishing, Quake Lake to Lyons Bridge and Ennis Bridge to Ennis Lake.
TROUT: Whirling disease has severely cut rainbow populations below Quake Lake but still a fair number in river; brown trout essentially unaffected. Middle river rainbows,10 to 16 inches; browns,14 to 18 inches. Browns over 24 inches lurk in Hebgen Lake, the upper river, below Varney Bridge.
MILES: 150 from Madison Junction in Yellowstone National Park to Missouri River. Mile 23: park boundary; Mile 40: Hebgen Dam; Mile 48.5: Quake Lake Slide; Mile 60: West Fork; Mile 77.5: McAtee Bridge; Mile 90: Varney Bridge; Mile 101.5: Ennis; Mile 112: Madison Dam; Mile 121.5: Highway 84 bridge; Mile 131: Grey Cliff; Mile 150: Missouri at Three Forks.
CHARACTER: Upper river meanders through marshy meadows to Hebgen Lake. Major white water, rapids in 2-mile stretch from Quake Lake to Madison Campground and through 9-mile Bear Trap Canyon below Ennis Lake. Middle river swift and shallow, basically a continuous riffle from Madison Campground to McAtee Bridge; deeper, with more boulders and pocket water down to Varney Bridge, where flows slow and meander down deep, undercut channels to Ennis Lake. Lower river runs through farmland.
FLOWS: Controlled by Hebgen and Madison dams; can be irregular. Middle river about 600 cubic feet per second, January to April; rises in May to 1,500 to 3,000 cfs in June; falls to about 900 cfs end of July; rises to about 1,400 cfs by September, and drops to about 900 cfs in December.
ACCESS: Many entry sites for waders on middle river along U.S. 287 and county roads. Comfortable floats from Madison Campground to Varney Bridge. Fewer access sites on lower river, which fishes best in spring, fall.
HATCHES: Caddis, late-April to October. Salmonfly, golden stones, late-June into July. Baetis, April-May, and October. PMD, June-August. Green drakes, Flavs, July into August. Grasshoppers, beetles, ants, July to October. Tricos, Callibaetis, late-July into September. Midges, spring and fall.
FLIES: Salmonfly, 2-6, golden stones, 6-8; caddis, stimulators, humpies, 10-16. BWO, PMD, Adams,16-22; green drake, 8-10; Flav, 12-16; trico, 18-22; Callibaetis, 14-16. Hoppers, 6-14. Beetles, 12-18. Ants, 14-22. Midge, 16-22. Stone nymphs, rubber-legs, woolly buggers, 2-10. Streamers, 2-8.

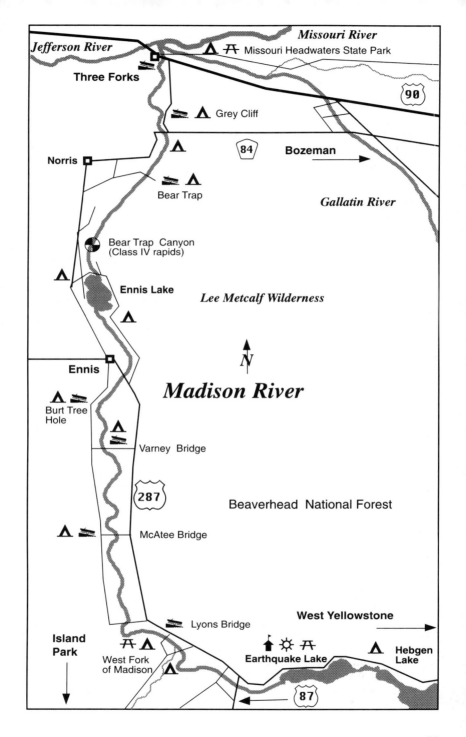

Missouri River

Jefferson River

Three Forks

△ ⊼ Missouri Headwaters State Park

Grey Cliff

Norris

84 → Bozeman

Bear Trap

Gallatin River

Bear Trap Canyon
(Class IV rapids)

Ennis Lake

Lee Metcalf Wilderness

N

Madison River

Ennis

Burt Tree Hole

Varney Bridge

287

Beaverhead National Forest

McAtee Bridge

West Yellowstone

Lyons Bridge

Island Park

West Fork of Madison

↑ ☼ ⊼
Earthquake Lake

△ Hebgen Lake

87

90

61

Yellowstone River

BEST FEATURES: Unspoiled legendary river with excellent public access in scenic, pastoral Paradise Valley. Good fishing opportunities, least crowded, before and after tourist season in early spring and late-fall.

SEASON: Open year-round.

REGULATIONS: Entire drainage: catch-and-release cutthroat trout. Main stem of river — except Emigrant bridge to Pine Creek bridge — 5-fish limit on rainbows and browns, only 1 over 18 inches. Emigrant bridge to Pine Creek bridge: 5 rainbows or browns, 4 under 13 inches, only 1 over 22 inches.

TROUT: Cutthroat, rainbows, browns in 12- to 16-inch class; chance for trophy fish, all species. Best cutthroat waters from Gardiner through Yankee Jim Canyon. Large browns most common below canyon to Pine Creek. Mostly rainbows, occasional trophy browns in lower Paradise Valley, Livingston to Big Timber. (Browns also run up Gardner River to spawn in fall.)

MILES: 678 from headwaters to Missouri River; 120 in park, 543 in Montana, 15 in North Dakota. Mile 120: Gardiner; Mile 131: Yankee Jim Canyon; Mile 135.5: Carbella; Mile 151: Emigrant; Mile 164.5: Mallard's Rest; Mile 179: Livingston; Mile 199: Springdale; and Mile 218: Big Timber.

CHARACTER: Upper run from Gardiner to Miner Creek is swift, rocky with deep runs, pools. Class IV rapids in Yankee Jim Canyon. Wide, big water river with braided channels through Paradise Valley but comfortable float for experienced boaters. Pace of river quickens at Pine Creek; dangerous hazard at 9th Street Bridge in Livingston. Many channels below Livingston.

FLOWS: Spring runoff starts in late-May, peaks between 15,000 and 20,000 cubic feet per second in June, falls rapidly through July to about 4,000 cfs in August. Late-fall flows below 3,000 cfs; winter, early spring flows often around 1,500 cfs. Summer storms in park can muddy water.

ACCESS: Numerous public access sites between Gardiner and Livingston; watch for signs on U.S. 89 and State Highway 540. Fewer public access sites, longer floats to pull-outs between Livingston and Big Timber. Best bet for waders is to work side channels, shallow runs, riffles, gravel bars and pools from public access sites in Paradise Valley and Livingston.

HATCHES: Baetis (BWO), late-March and April. Caddis, April and May. Salmon fly, July. Golden stones, yellow Sallies, July and mid-August. Western green drake, early July. Caddis and mayflies (PMD), mid-summer. Grass-hoppers, August and September. Baetis, late-fall. Midges, winter.

FLIES: BWO, blue dun, PMD, 16-22; green drake, 10-12; Adams, Cahill, renegade, 14-18; elk hair caddis, yellow Sallies, stimulators, humpies, Wulffs, Trudes, 10-14; salmon fly, 4-8; golden stone, 6-8; grasshoppers, 6-10. Hare's ear, pheasant tail, prince, soft-hackle nymphs, 10-16. Dark stone fly nymphs, rubber-legs, woolly buggers, crystal buggers, 2-10. Muddlers, wool-head sculpin, Matuka streamers, Zonkers, spruce flies, 2-4.

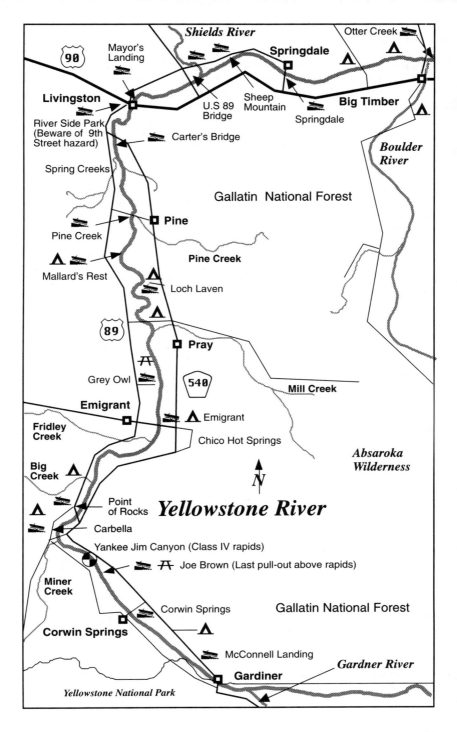

90

Shields River

Otter Creek

Mayor's Landing

Springdale

Livingston

U.S 89 Bridge

Sheep Mountain

Big Timber

River Side Park (Beware of 9th Street hazard)

Springdale

Carter's Bridge

Boulder River

Spring Creeks

Gallatin National Forest

Pine

Pine Creek

Pine Creek

Mallard's Rest

Loch Laven

89

Pray

Grey Owl

540

Mill Creek

Emigrant

Emigrant

Fridley Creek

Chico Hot Springs

Absaroka Wilderness

Big Creek

Point of Rocks

N

Yellowstone River

Carbella

Yankee Jim Canyon (Class IV rapids)

Miner Creek

Joe Brown (Last pull-out above rapids)

Corwin Springs

Gallatin National Forest

Corwin Springs

McConnell Landing

Gardner River

Gardiner

Yellowstone National Park

Boulder River

BEST FEATURES: High mountain stream with headwaters in alpine "roof of Montana," the Absaroka-Beartooth Wilderness. Its two main tributaries, East Boulder and West Boulder, offer excellent fishing. Over the ridge to the east is the Stillwater River, a carbon-copy of the Boulder.

SEASON: Entire drainage, including tributaries, open year-round.

REGULATIONS: Lower river, below Natural Bridge Falls, 2-trout limit, only 1 over 13 inches. Natural Bridge Falls to Two Mile Bridge, catch-and-release for rainbows; artificial flies and lures only.

TROUT: Boulder River has rainbow and brook trout above falls; rainbows and browns below falls. East Boulder has strong population of cutthroat, and a few rainbows at top. West Boulder has rainbows and browns above its confluence, and rainbows, cutthroat and brook trout in high country waters.

MILES: 62 miles from headwaters to Yellowstone River. Mile 2: Two-mile Bridge; Mile 5: Box Canyon (road's end); Mile 12: Hells Canyon; Mile 26: Boulder Ranger Station; Mile 29: Natural Bridge Falls; Mile 39: East Boulder; Mile 43: West Boulder; Mile 57: Big Rock; Mile 62: Big Timber.

CHARACTER: Beautiful, classic mountain stream that tumbles and plunges through boulder-strewn cascades and fast riffles, with numerous pools, pocket waters and cutbanks. Irrigation diversions on lower stretch. Drops from elevation of 8,800 feet to 4,000 at mouth. Difficult to wade due to numerous boulders, slippery rocks. Natural Bridge Falls is 105 feet high.

FLOWS: Spring runoff begins in mid-April, peaks around 3,000 cubic feet per second by June, falls rapidly to around 1,000 cfs by July and to 500 cfs by August. Late-fall and early spring flows hover around 400 to 500 cfs.

ACCESS: Mostly private land along lower 30 miles of river and on some in-holdings above Gallatin National Forest boundary. Several bridge access sites in lower river and at Big Rock Campground. Paved county road to falls and gravel road upstream hug river 57 miles to Box Canyon. Gravel roads also parallel both forks upstream to forest boundary. Trail at Box Canyon follows upper river and crosses divide to Slough Creek and Yellowstone National Park. This is also a key starting point for hikes into the western Beartooth Wilderness. Numerous dude ranches on lower river.

HATCHES: Good stone fly hatch begins around mid-June. In early spring through mid-summer look for golden stones, caddis, willow flies and mayflies, including small white-wing sulphur known as the yellow drake. Grasshoppers, ants and beetles are very effective August and September.

FLIES: Stone fly, 4-8. Tan, brown and olive elk hair caddis, yellow and orange stimulators or humpies, yellow Sally, 12-16. PMD, BWO, Adams, Wulffs, renegades, 14 -18. Yellow drake, 10-12. Grasshoppers, 6-12. Ants, beetles, 14-18. Stonefly nymphs, rubber-legs, woolly buggers, 4-10. Fish caddis emergers, prince and hare's ear nymphs, 12-16, as dropper flies.

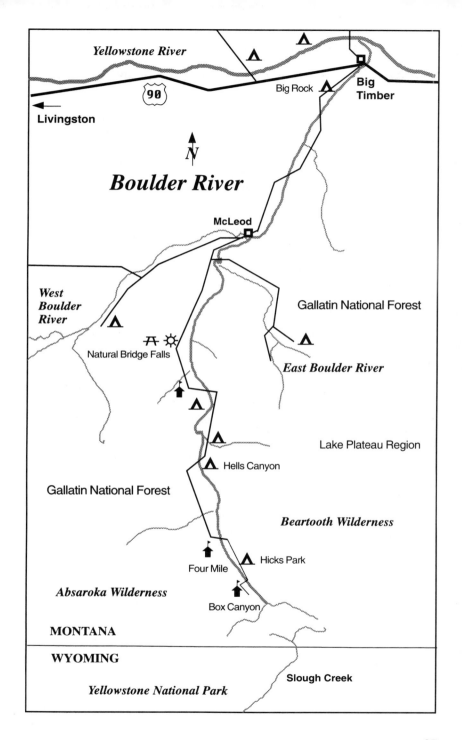

Yellowstone River

90

← Livingston

N

Boulder River

Big Rock

Big Timber

McLeod

West Boulder River

Gallatin National Forest

Natural Bridge Falls

East Boulder River

Lake Plateau Region

Hells Canyon

Gallatin National Forest

Beartooth Wilderness

Four Mile

Hicks Park

Absaroka Wilderness

Box Canyon

MONTANA

WYOMING

Slough Creek

Yellowstone National Park

65

Other adventures:

The Spring Creeks and Beartooth-Absaroka lakes

Test your mettle on idyllic spring creeks:
Analytical fishing types who want to savor the quintessential fine arts of fly fishing will find the challenges they seek in serene settings on two privately owned tributaries of the Yellowstone River. Turn south at Livingston and sign up as a "rod" for graduate school tests in mental fishing at one of three pay-to-fish spring creek retreats.

Six miles south on U.S. 89 on the west side of the Yellowstone is DePuy's Spring Creek (Call of the Wild Ranch). The turnoff to O'Hair's (Armstrong) Spring Creek is just past Mile Marker 47. They share Armstrong Creek. Downstream and across the river is Nelson's Spring Creek. Prices range from $75 to $50 a day in summer, to $25 during the off-season.

The payback is technical fishing for large, smart fish in shallow crystal clear waters. Be prepared to read the water, match the hatch — or stages of the hatch. Follow through with precision casting and finite fly presentation. Most anglers key on the hefty rainbows and browns, but native cutthroat also reside in these internationally acclaimed spring creeks. And, since major improvements in stream access in the early 1990s at DePuy's, Armstrong Creek has joined Nelson's Spring Creek as an essential spawning stream for the lower Yellowstone's rainbows.

Reservations are required and, usually, there is a long waiting list. Cancellations occur, however. When in the area, it is worth calling to see if you can squeeze into a golden opportunity. Better yet, plan a visit in early spring or late-fall when crowds are less of a problem.

■ DePuy's Spring Creek, Route 38, Box 2267, Livingston, MT 59047; 1-406-222-0221; 15 rods per day, $50, April 15 to Oct. 14; $25 rest of year.

■ O'Hair's Spring Creek, P.O. Box 955, Livingston, MT 59047; 1-406-222-2979; 10-12 rods per day, $50, April 1 to Aug. 31; $25 in off-season.

■ Nelson's Spring Creek, 90 Nelson's Spring Creek Road, Livingston, MT 59047; 1-406-222-2159; 6 rods per day, $75, April 1 to Nov. 1; $25 in off-season.

Alpine lakes wonderland:
At the top of the greater Yellowstone ecosystem is the Absaroka-Beartooth Wilderness, "the roof of Montana." Scattered like emeralds across this high, broad plateau are 1,000 lakes; more than 430 hold trout or grayling. Above timberline, most are at 8,500 feet or higher. Marker Lake, the highest, basks in the rarefied air of 10,870 feet.

The fabulous alpine scenery draws hundreds of adventurous souls with iron lungs and steel thighs. For fly fishers, brilliant iridescent trout in a lake at trail's end make all the huffing and puffing worth the effort. For a fortunate few, the ultimate reward is a lake with a hatch in progress, dimpled with hundreds of concentric circles from the rise-forms of feeding fish. The species list for the multitude of lakes and streams ranges from native cutthroat to brook, rainbow and golden trout to grayling. Sizes vary with lake conditions and fish populations. Most are small, but be prepared for surprises. Ice out on the higher lakes generally occurs in late June or early July.

Fly choices are very basic for high mountain lakes and streams. Dry fly action is limited in mid-summer, so plan on mostly working the lakes with wet flies. Concentrate on shorelines and shallows and use a dropper fly to speed up prospecting. Dry flies include the standard mayfly, caddis, midge and small terrestrial patterns. The most common mayfly in lakes is the Callibaetis. Attractor patterns include Adams, renegades, ants, beetles, humpies, stimulators, royal Wulffs and Coachmans. Wet flies for high lakes range from leech patterns, small streamers and woolly buggers to beadhead nymphs, Chironomid or green midge pupa, soft-hackle nymphs, Carey Special, prince nymph, hare's ear, green caddis emerger, peacock emerger and pheasant tail to green scud and gray or green shrimp patterns.

Rod choices depend on conditions or length of the hike into a lake. A three-piece, 8-foot 5- or 6-weight travel rod with a weight-forward or floating line and medium sinking tip is handy on longer trips. Big lakes or windy conditions may require a 9-foot 6- or 7-weight rod.

At these elevations snow can occur any time of the year. Pack for early spring or fall-like conditions even in mid-summer. Summer squalls, sometimes accompanied by intense lightning, are common and can drop temperatures 20 degrees. Always include rain gear, a sweater, wool socks, knit cap and gloves or mittens in your day pack. Don't forget insect repellent. Take note, too, that this is grizzly bear country. Never hike alone — groups of 3 or 4 are recommended — and keep a clean camp.

Plan a minimum of three days for really high or remote lakes. Maps are available from the Custer National Forest. Topographical maps help to plan extended hikes or determine elevation gains of shorter ones. "Beartooth Fishing Guide" by Pat Marcuson and "The Trail Guide to the Beartooths" by Bill Schneider are available from Falcon Press, Helena, MT.

The Boulder River divides the alpine wilderness, with the Absaroka Mountains on the west and the Beartooth Mountains on the east. Trailheads at the top of the Boulder and East Boulder roads lead to the western Beartooth Wilderness. The West Boulder road leads into the eastern Absaroka Wilderness. Turn south at Big Timber to reach these trailheads.

To reach the top of the Beartooth Wilderness fast, take U.S. 212 from Red Lodge to Cooke City over the Beartooth Scenic Highway. Other Beartooth trailheads are in the Stillwater River and Rosebud Creek drainages southwest of Columbus, Rock Creek drainage southwest of Red Lodge, and Clark's Fork drainage northeast of Cooke City.

Visitor Information

IDAHO:

Travel information: 1-800-VISIT ID
- Idaho Travel Department
700 W. State Street, 2nd Floor Boise, ID 83720
1-208-334-2470
- Idaho State Parks and Recreation
P.O. Box 83720 Boise, ID 83720-0065
1-208-334-4199
Fishing updates: 1-800-ASK FISH
- Idaho Fish and Game
P.O. Box 25, Boise, ID 83707
1-208-334-3700
- Idaho Fish and Game
1515 Lincoln Road, Idaho Falls, ID 83401
1-208-525-7290
- Idaho Fish and Game
1345 Barton Road, Pocatello, ID 83204
1-208-232-4703
- Harriman State Park
South of Island Park
1-208-558-7368
- Henry's Lake State Park
North of Island Park
1-208-558-7532
- Targhee National Forest
Supervisor's Office
420 N. Bridge, St. Anthony, ID
1-208-624-3151
Information recording: 1-208-624-4576
- Palisades Ranger District
3659 E. Ririe Highway. (U.S. 26), Idaho Falls, ID 83401
1-208-523-1412
- Visitor Information Center (USFS, BLM, city of Idaho Falls)
505 Lindsay Blvd., Idaho Falls, ID 83402
1-208-523-3278
- Bureau of Land Management
1405 Hollipark Drive, Idaho Falls, ID 83401
1-208-525-7500
- Fort Hall Indian Reservation Tribal Fish and Game Department, southwest of Blackfoot, ID
1-208-238-3743

MONTANA:
Travel information: 1-800-VISIT MT, ext. 508
- Montana Travel Department
1424 9th Avenue, Helena, MT 59620
1-406-444-2654

- Yellowstone Country
P.O. Box 1107, Red Lodge, MT 59068
1-406-446-1105 1-800-736-5276
- Montana Department of Fish, Wildlife & Parks
1420 E. Sixth Avenue, Helena, MT 59620
1-406-444-2535
- Fish, Wildlife & Parks Region 3
1400 South 19th, Bozeman, MT 59715
1-406-994-4042
- Gallatin National Forest
P.O. Box 130, Bozeman, MT 59771
1-406-587-6701
- Gallatin National Forest
West Yellowstone, MT
1-406-646-7369

WYOMING:
Travel information: 1-800-225-5996
- Wyoming Division of Tourism
I-25 at College Drive, Cheyenne, WY 82002-0660
1-307-777-7777
- Wyoming Game and Fish
5400 Bishop Blvd., Cheyenne, WY 82006
1-307-777-7014
- Wyoming Game and Fish
360 N. Cache, Jackson, WY
1-307-733-2321
- Wyoming Game and Fish
2820 Highway. 120, Cody, WY
1-307-527-7125
- Bridger-Teton National Forest
P.O. Box 1888, Jackson, WY 83001
1-307-733-2752
- Bureau of Land Management
P.O. Box 1828, Cheyenne, WY 82003
1-307-722-2334

NATIONAL PARKS

- Yellowstone National Park
P.O. Box 168
Attn. Visitor's Service
Yellowstone National Park, WY 82190
1-307-344-7381
- TW Recreational Services (lodging reservations)
P.O. Box 165, Yellowstone National Park, WY 82190-0165
1-307-344-7311
- Grand Teton National Park
P.O. Drawer 170, Moose, WY 83012-0170
1-307-739-3399
Visitor information: 1-307-733-3600

River and back country information (recorded): 1-307-739-3602
■ Grand Teton Lodge Co. (lodging reservations)
P.O. Box 240, Moran, WY 83013
1-307-543-2855

Chambers of Commerce

- ■ Idaho Falls, ID   1-208-523-1010
- ■ Island Park, ID 1-800-543-1895
- ■ Ashton, ID (city hall) 1-208-652-3987
- ■ St. Anthony, ID (city hall) 1-208-624-3494
- ■ Driggs, ID   1-208-354-2500
- ■ Jackson, WY   1-307-733-3316
- ■ Cody, WY   1-307-587-2297
- ■ Dubois, WY   1-307-455-2556
- ■ West Yellowstone, MT   1-406-646-7701
- ■ Bozeman, MT   1-406-586-5421
- ■ Livingston, MT   1-406-222-0850
- ■ Gardiner, MT   1-406-848-7971
- ■ Cooke City, MT   1-406-838-2251
- ■ Red Lodge, MT   1-406-446-1718

Outfitters / Fly Shops

(Note: Majority of outfitters have fly shops)

IDAHO:
■ Idaho Outfitters and Guides Association
P.O. Box 95, Boise, ID 83701
1-208-342-1438
For free directory: 1-800-847-4843
■ Heise Expeditions
5089 E. Heise Road, Ririe, ID 83443
1-208-538-5081
(South Fork of Snake River)
■ Henry's Fork Anglers
HC 66 Box 491, Island Park, ID 83429
1-208-558-7525 / 1-208-624-3590 / 1-800-788-4479
(Henry's Fork of Snake River, Henry's Lake, Island Park Reservoir;
Madison River, Yellowstone Park)
■ Hyde Outfitters, Pro Fly Shop and Drift Boats
1520 Pancheri, Idaho Falls, ID 83402
1-208-529-4343 / 1-800-444-4933
(South Fork of Snake River, Teton River, Palisades Reservoir)
■ Jimmy's All Seasons Angler Fly Shop
275 A Street, Idaho Falls, ID 83402
1-208-524-7160
■ B&B Drugs and Fly Shop
2425 Channing Way, Idaho Falls, ID 83402
1-208-523-2277

- Gart Sports
2090 N. Yellowstone Highway, Idaho Falls, ID 83401
1-208-524-2525
- Last Chance Outfitters
HC 66 Box 482, Island Park, ID 83429
1-208-558-7068
(Henry's Fork of Snake River, Henry's Lake, Island Park Reservoir)
- The Lodge at Palisades Creek
Box 70, Irwin, ID 83428
1-208-483-2222
(South Fork of Snake River, Henry's Fork of Snake River)
- Sandy Mite Fly Shop
3333 Swan Valley Highway, Irwin, ID 83428
1-208-483-2609
- Laren M. Piquet
483 West Bates Road, Driggs, ID 83422
1-208-354-2786
(Teton River)
- Harrop Flies
33 W 4 Street North, St. Anthony, ID
1-208-624-3537
- Frontier Tackle & Gear
30 S. Bridge Street, St. Anthony, ID 83445
1-208-624-3975
- BS Flies & Tackle
Valley View, ID (Henry's Lake)
1-208-558-7879 (summer) / 1-208-356-7275 (winter)
(Henry's Lake, Island Park Reservoir)
- South Fork Expeditions
Box 2584, Idaho Falls, ID 83403
1-208-483-2722 / 1-208-483-2060
(South Fork of Snake River, Palisades Reservoir)
- South Fork Lodge
Box 22, Swan Valley, ID 83449
1-208-483-2112 / 1-800-483-2110
(South Fork of Snake River)
- Teton Valley Lodge
379 Adams Road, Driggs, ID 83422
1-208-354-2386 / 1-208-354-8124
(Teton River, South Fork, Henry's Fork, Island Park Reservoir)
- Three Rivers Ranch
Box 856 Warm River, Ashton, ID 83420
1-208-652-3750 / FAX 1-208-652-3788
(Teton River, South Fork, Henry's Fork, Henry's Lake, Island Park Res.)

MONTANA:
- Fishing Outfitters Association of Montana
Box 67, Gallatin Gateway, MT 59730
1-406-763-4761

■ Bud Lily's Trout Shop
39 Madison Avenue, West Yellowstone, MT 59758
1-406-646-7801 / FAX 1-406-646-9370
(Madison, Gallatin, Yellowstone Park; Henry's Fork, Henry's Lake)
■ Jacklin's Outfitters For World of Fly Fishing
105 Yellowstone Avenue, West Yellowstone, MT 59758
1-406-646-7336 / FAX 1-406-646-9729
(Madison, Gallatin, Yellowstone Park; Henry's Fork, Henry's Lake)
■ Yellowstone Catch & Release Outfitters
127 Dunravan, West Yellowstone, MT 59758
1-406-646-9082
■ Arrick's Fishing Flies
128 Madison Avenue, West Yellowstone, MT 59758
1-406-646-7290
■ Blue Ribbon Flies
315 Canyon, West Yellowstone MT 59758
1-406-646-7642
■ Madison River Outfitters
117 Canyon, West Yellowstone, MT 59758
1-406-646-9644
■ East Slope Anglers
Highway 191, Big Sky, MT 59716
1-406-995-4369
■ Gallatin Riverguides
Highway 191, Box 160212, Big Sky, MT 59716
1-406-995-2290
(Gallatin , Madison, Yellowstone, Missouri rivers)
■ Wild Trout Outfitters
302 Guest Ranch, Big Sky, MT 59716
1-406-995-4895
(Gallatin, Madison, Yellowstone rivers)
■ Lone Mountain Ranch
Big Sky, MT 59716
1-406-995-4644
(Madison and Gallatin rivers, Yellowstone Park)
■ Beartooth Flyfishing
2975 Highway 267, N. Cameron, Bozeman, MT 59715
1-406-682-7525
■ Montana Troutfitters
1716 W. Main, Bozeman, MT 59715
1-406-587-4707
■ The River's Edge
2012 N. 7th Avenue, Bozeman, MT 59715
1-406-586-5373
■ RJ Cain & Co. Outfitters
24 E. Main St., Bozeman, MT 59715
1-406-587-9111
Box 150, Ennis, MT 59729
1-406-682-7451
■ Madison River Fishing Company
109 Main Street, Box 627, Ennis, MT 59729
1-406-682-4293

■ Headwaters Anglers & Adventure Center
Gardiner, MT
1-406-848-7110
■ Park's Fly Shop
Gardiner, MT
1-406-848-7314
■ Anderson's Yellowstone Anglers
Highway 89 South of Livingston, MT
1-406-222-7130
■ Dan Bailey's
209 W. Park, Livingston, MT
1-406-1673 / 1-800-356-4052
■ Adventures Out West
1515 W. Park, Livingston, MT
1-406-222-2100
■ Montana's Master Angler
107 S. Main, Livingston, MT
1-406-222-2273
■ Yellowstone's International Fly Fisherman's Lodge
South of Livingston, MT
1-406-333-4787
■ Wilderness Outfitters
Highway 89 South of Livingston, MT
1-406-222-6933
■ Big Sky Flies & Guides
Highway 89, Emigrant, MT 59027
1-406-333-4401
■ Beartooth Plateau Outfitters
Cooke City, MT
1-800-253-8545

WYOMING:
■ Wyoming Outfitters Association
Box 2284
Cody, WY 82414
1-307-527-7453
■ Bressler Outfitter
Box 766, Wilson, WY 83014
1-307-733-6934 / 1-800-654-0676
(South Fork of Snake River, Teton River in Idaho)
■ Fort Jackson Fishing Expeditions
Jackson, WY
1-307-733-2583 / 1-800-735-8430
■ Flagg Ranch
South Entrance of Yellowstone National Park
1-307-543-2861
■ Jack Dennis Outdoor Shop
50 E. Broadway, Jackson, WY
1-307-733-3270
■ Joe Allen's Scenic Fishing
300 Flat Creek Drive, Jackson, WY
1-307-733-2400 / 1-800-807-2920

- Lazy B River Company
Jackson Hole, WY
1-307-733-0759
- Reel Women Fly Fishing Adventures
2450 Shooting Iron Road,
Jackson, WY
1-307-733-2210
- Mill Iron Ranch
Box 951, Jackson, WY
1-307-733-6390
- Signal Mountain Lodge
Grand Teton National Park, Jackson, WY
1-307-543-2831
- Westbank Anglers
Box 523 Dept. USW, Teton Village, WY 83205
1-307-733-6483 / 1-800-922-3474
- Orvis of Jackson
485 W. Broadway, Jackson, WY
1-307-733-5407
- Wyoming Outfitter's High Country Flies
165 Center Street, Jackson, WY
1-307-733-7210
- B G's Alpine Merc
Alpine, WY 83120
1-307-654-7509
- The Tackle Box
Alpine, WY 83110
1-307-654-7762
- Star Valley Trout Ranch
Box 1266, Afton, WY
1-307-225-3543
- Aune's Absoroka Angler
1390 Sheridan Avenue, Cody, WY
1-307-587-5105
- North Fork Anglers
937 Sheridan Avenue, Cody, WY
1-307-527-7274
- Yellowstone Troutfitters
239 Yellowstone Avenue, Cody, WY
1-307-587-8240

Fishing seasons / License fees

YELLOWSTONE NATIONAL PARK:

Season: Fishing is open Saturday of Memorial Day weekend through October 31, except where specifically restricted. Check park regulations.

Fees: Anglers over 16 need $10 ten-day permit or $20 season permit. Anglers 12-15 can obtain free permit. A $20 annual or $10 seven-day permit is required for motorized boats; $10 annual or $5 seven-day permit for non-motorized boats. (Boats permitted only on designated lakes; no boats on streams.)

Note: Yellowstone is a lead-free fishing zone. No lead sinkers and jigs or lead-weighted flies are permitted. Non-toxic options are available. Purpose of ban is to prevent swans and other birds from dying of lead poisoning.

WYOMING:

Season: Fishing is open year-round except for specifically designated waters and drainages. Check Wyoming Game and Fish regulations.

Fees: Resident license fee is $10, plus a $5 conservation stamp. License for youth between 14 and 19 years of age is $3, plus $5 conservation stamp. No license required under age 14. Tourist fishing license fee is $60 for a season, plus a $5 conservation stamp. The fee for out-of-state youth between 14 and 19 is $15 for an annual license. or $10 for a 10-day license. One-day license for a resident is $3 per day and $6 per day for a tourist. A fishing license for military personnel is $10. NOTE: Wyoming fishing license required for Grand Teton National Park.

IDAHO:

Season: General fishing season is from Saturday of Memorial Day weekend through November 30 except where specifically restricted. Most lakes and a few designated river stretches are open year-round. Check Idaho Fish and Game regulations.

Fees: Resident license fee is $16.50 for ages 18 to 64, $5.50 for ages 65 to 69, and free for anglers 70 and older. Youth license is $8.50 for ages 14 to 17. Tourist license is $51.50 for season. Single-day fishing permit for resident or tourist is $7.50 for first day, plus $3 for each additional day.

MONTANA:

Season: General fishing season in western and central Montana for most rivers and streams is third Saturday in May through November 30. Some rivers and most lakes are open year-round. Check Montana Fish, Wildlife and Parks regulations for year-round or whitefish seasons on specific streams.

Fees: Resident fishing license is $13, plus a $4 conservation license. Residents ages 12 to 14 and 62 and older only need $4 conservation license. Tourist license is $52 for season, $10 for two days, plus a $5 non-resident conservation license.

Trout Identification

Rainbow trout
(Oncorhycus mykiss)

The most exciting fighter of the trout family, you can always count on a tussle from the rainbow. It was reclassified as part of the western salmon genus *(Oncorhycus)* in 1990; former classification was with Atlantic salmon genus *(Salmo)*. A West Coast species, it was introduced into Yellowstone country in 1880s. Its common name comes from broad swath of crimson to pinkish-red usually seen along midline of its flanks. Reddish band may be absent in lake dwellers, which are generally more silver in total appearance. River rainbow coloration ranges from olive to greenish-blue on back, with white to silvery belly. Marked with many irregular black spots on head, back and tail, and extending below midline. **Best waters:** Henry's Fork; Madison River.

Yellowstone cutthroat trout
(Oncorhycus clarki bouvieri)

The dry fly purist's favorite trout, the cutthroat's lusty rises are always exciting. Its fight is usually below water and stubborn, using stream flows to its advantage, but often short-lived. It was reclassified as part of the western salmon genus *(Oncorhycus)* in 1990; former classification was with Atlantic salmon genus *(Salmo)*. Its common name comes from orange-red slash marks under lower jaw. Body coloration ranges from silver-gray to olive-green back, with yellow-brown flanks, orange-tinted fins and reddish gill-plates. Spots fewer, larger and more round than rainbow, and less dense on tail. Cutthroat-rainbow hybrids display most of rainbow's coloration, spotting; throat slashes light-orange to almost indistinct. **Best waters:** Yellowstone River, Yellowstone Lake; Henry's Lake, South Fork of the Snake.

Snake River finespotted cutthroat trout
(Oncorhycus clarki sp)

Characteristics same as Yellowstone cutthroat, with denser spotting pattern more similar to coastal species than interior cutthroat. Body coloration more subtle; overlay of many fine spots concentrating toward tail and extending below midline. Tail and lower fins sometimes darker orange. **Best waters:** Snake River in Wyo.

Brown trout
(Salmo trutta)

The brown trout's reputation for wariness is well deserved, although it rises well to a dry fly when the hatch is "profitable." Its run is often long and deep, and refuses to come to the net peacefully.

Longer-lived than North American species, it can grow to trophy size. Its scientific name declares it as the "true trout." It was introduced into Yellowstone country in the late-1880s from stocks originating in Scotland and Germany. Coloration is generally golden-brown; back dark-brown to greenish-brown, belly ranging to lemon-yellow. Spaced-out, large black or brown spots, mixed with few red spots on sides with light halos. Few or no spots on squarish tail. **Best waters:** South Fork of Snake; Hebgen Lake; lower Yellowstone River.

Brook trout
(Salvelinus fortinalis)

The brook trout is a scrappy fighter, but most western anglers find it only in a diminutive size, stunted from over population. Attempts to create trophy populations, such as in Henry's Lake, have had mixed success. An East Coast species, the brookie, like the lake trout, is a char common to eastern U.S. and Canadian waters. Most distinctive marking is white and black edges on fronts of lower fins, and wavy or mottled markings on back. Overall color darker olive-green than western species. Introduced into West in 1880s. **Best waters:** Henry's Lake, alpine lakes.

Catch-and-release tips

All anglers can help make future fishing better by releasing wild trout. Flies with only one barbless hook make release of fish easier.

Catch and release fish through the following procedures:

1. Use the strongest terminal tackle conditions permit to make the landing battle as short as possible.

2. Land fish with net with fine, soft mesh.

3. Wet hands before touching the fish. Do not squeeze it.

4. Do not touch the gills or hold fish by gill covers.

5. If possible, leave the fish in the water while removing the hook. Use of needle-nose pliers or medical forceps is recommended. Work quickly but gently.

6. If the hook cannot be easily removed, cut the leader. The hook will rust out rapidly.

7. Do not toss fish back into water or shake fish off hook by suspending it in mid-air. Turn over mouth of net to let it escape or lean over side of boat to slide it gently into water.

8. If the fish is exhausted, hold it in a swimming position in the water and move gently back and forth to force water through gills. Maintain light grip on tail until it pulls itself out of your hands and swims off on its own.

9. Avoid excessive and unnecessary handling of the fish, especially when taking photographs.

■

"Fly fishing is the classiest chess game in town and we must be chivalrous enough to leave the pieces on the board so that others can play — catch and release is the only way to ensure the quality of the sport."

Sheridan Anderson,
"The Curtis Creek Manifesto"

Stream Notes:

Order Form

Greater Yellowstone Fly Fisher's Stream Guide $14.95
Fly Fisher's Guide to Idaho $26.95
Mail to:
     Ken Retallic
     190 S. Corner Street
     Idaho Falls, ID 83402   Phone: (208) 523-7539

Quantity   _____

Book Title   _____

Price   _____

Sub total   _____

Idaho Residents add 5 % sales tax

Shipping & handling: $4 for one book, $2.50 each additional book

Total   _____

(For retail sales, call for wholesale rates.)

Make payment by check or money order and mail to above address.
Allow 2 to 4 weeks for delivery.

Your address: Phone: _____

     Name _____

     Address _____

     City _____

     State/Zip Code _____

Gift Mail to:

     Name _____

     Address _____

     City _____

     State/Zip Code _____